THE ELEMENTS OF

MYSTICISM

R A Gilbert

ELEMENT BOOKS

Published in Great Britain in 1991 by
Element Books Limited
Longmead, Shaftesbury, Dorset

Published in the USA in 1991 by
Element Inc
42 Broadway, Rockport, MA 01966

Cover design by Max Fairbrother
Typeset by Selectmove Ltd, London
Printed and bound in Great Britain by
Billings Ltd, Hylton Road, Worcester

British Library Cataloguing in Publication Data
Gilbert, R. A.
The elements of mysticism.
1. Mysticism
I. Title
149.3

ISBN 1–85230–201–1

CONTENTS

**To the Memory
of
M.C.D.**

PREFACE

Books on mysticism are, like leaves in Vallombrosa,[1] without number; why, then, do I add another? I cannot offer anything that is radically different from what has gone before, because the reality that lies behind the mystical experience does not change, however much we may alter our way of speaking about it.

But precisely because the subtle interplay of language and cultural change leads to a constant shifting of the manner in which we express our understanding of both temporal and spiritual realities, we cannot expect critical studies of mysticism to retain their clarity and popular appeal for ever. The descriptions, insights and interpretations that they contain need to be presented anew as the new patterns into which society moulds itself become clearly defined: it is with this in mind that I offer my brief overview of the subject.

Apart from the many texts and translations of the mystics themselves that are currently available, works on mysticism abound: some of the classic studies are in print, but many more are not, and much that is to be found consists of scholarly studies on individual authors, or on specific themes in mystical literature, or on particular approaches to interpreting the subject. What remains are handbooks of the do-it-yourself kind – rich in woolly thought and flowery language, but poor in both reason and practicality – and devotional anthologies that are devoted primarily to the peculiar notions of their editors. I have aspired to be none of these, endeavouring instead to present what is sorely needed – a general introduction to mysticism that is neither highly technical nor doctrinaire, but is yet both comprehensive and concise.

Even so, I am painfully aware that I cannot succeed in being all things to all men and that neither the structure nor the content of this book will satisfy all. Beginning with an attempt to pin down the meaning of mysticism – a notoriously slippery word – I have tried to chart the progress of the mystic and his work down the ages and in many different faiths. And here I must point out that while I have consistently used 'he' and 'his' throughout my text when referring to the mystics themselves, this is simply for convenience and brevity; I know that there are as many female mystics as male, and that no distinction should be drawn between them – on grounds of sex – in terms either of their spirituality or their literary quality.

But the very word 'spirituality' betrays a specific approach to mysticism, and I have also outlined the forms of mysticism that are not theistic, together with those other forms that are either aberrations or that have slipped into common acceptance as 'mysticism' by way of a definition of the word that is very elastic indeed. All of which, necessary though it is, may be seen as a long introduction to a much briefer but – so I believe – more essential core.

Many books on mysticism do not take their consideration of just what it is beyond expanded definitions of its various forms. If we are to understand it, then we must know not only to what the words in our definitions refer, but also how the mystical experience itself is mediated within us. To this end I have offered an analysis of the experience, drawing on psychological and neurophysiological research as well as on the work of philosophers and theologians (whose exclusive province it has usually, if short-sightedly, been taken to be.)

It cannot be a complete and final analysis, for we still know all too little about the workings of the brain, and even less about the nature of human consciousness. And there are other problems, notably the lack of agreement among both mystics and their interpreters as to the precise meaning of many of the words they use: what consensus of opinion is there among medieval and modern mystics, and between Christian mystics and those of other faiths as to the meaning of Mind (for example)? The answer is little or none, and it is awareness of this problem that has led me to tread very warily when considering the question that next arises: how does the mystic communicate the nature and content of his experience to others? The answer to this lies in territory that is almost wholly unexplored and I cannot pretend to have done more than to have travelled a little way and to have erected a signpost for the benefit of those who follow.

And if the mystics have aspired to and attained the direct experience of God, or the Absolute, or Ultimate Reality, can we also attain it? We can at least try to attain, and I have brought the book to its close by suggesting various paths that might be pursued in our search for the Way to Attainment. Not all of them will be appropriate for everyone, and it is for the reader to determine which, if any of them, is best suited to his individual being. He might also ask what right I have to put them forward as valid paths: have I tried them? Have I experienced the mystical state? Indeed, am I a mystic?

To these questions I can answer only: no, I am not a mystic; but, yes, I have tried these paths of attainment; and – to the question of having experienced the mystical state – perhaps. I will explain. Our perception and immediate understanding of all religious experiences is conditioned by our cultural background and coloured by our personal faith. In my case I have grown up in the nominally Christian environment that prevails in Britain in the second half of the twentieth century. By personal conviction I am and remain a Christian, albeit no longer confessionally committed to a specific denomination, and my experiences reflect my faith: such numinous states as I have known have been experienced in the context of Christian prayer, ceremony and meditation (although the latter has been within a Kabbalistic group concerned with a Christian understanding of the Tree of Life.)

On one occasion, in Oxford Cathedral, I was aware of an exaltation quite different from anything induced by sensory pleasure or by its anticipation. I was in the presence of something much greater than myself: awe-inspiring and at the same time loving. There was no name to it, and no immediate label sprang to mind, so that I cannot say that it was the presence of Christ, only that it may have been. My other experiences have come in the course of meditation, within a Christian Kabbalistic context, and those familiar with Kabbalistic terminology will understand when I say that the only way of describing them is that they were a consciousness of Daath in Briah.[2]

It is not easy to transfer this into other words. All that I can say is that I retained no memory of the content of the experience, only the certain knowledge that I had been in that state in which, to use the words of a contemporary Christian Kabbalist,[3] 'we receive the highest possible benediction in this world.' Beyond that simple statement there is nothing to be said as far as the experience goes: I was in that state and then I was no longer in it, but left with an awareness of what had been.

But did it make me a better person? In the moral sense as usually understood, I would answer 'No', but it unquestionably changed me. The will to attain the mystic state has remained with me, and with it the desire to bring to others a knowledge of the experience – and of the certainty of a Reality that lies beyond the world of our senses. Whether this certainty can be conveyed in ordinary language is doubtful, but even if the immediate sense of the words cannot be adequately transmitted, something else may pass from one to another. What St Augustine said of the Christian scriptures may be applied to what the mystic tries to communicate: 'What harm is there if a reader believes what you, the light of all truthful minds, show him to be the true meaning? It may not even be the meaning which the writer had in mind, and yet he too saw a true meaning, different though it may have been from this.'

And I have not confined myself to the words of Christian mystics, for whatever faith the mystic is born in and writes in, it is the same reality that he has known. There is a common thread running through the spiritual experiences of

Hindu, Buddhist, Gnostic, Sufi, Kabbalist and Christian, and it suffuses all that they have written – however disparate their styles and however seemingly irreconcileable their doctrinal stances. It is the elusive essence of this thread that I have tried to catch in order to illustrate the true nature of the mystic's experience of Reality.

Many of the texts I have quoted may be well known to the reader, but I have included others whose unfamiliarity stems in part from the difficulty of their language, and in part from their unorthodoxy. Because he travels directly to the presence of God, the mystic passes behind the doctrinal structures of his outward faith and often he finds that those structures do not correspond to his understanding of the Reality they are supposed to explain. If he is discreet he will keep his views to himself, but if not he will be treated as a heretic and, at best, face censure or, more probably, persecution – as did Jacob Boehme. Some mystics, such as the Sufi al-Hallaj, have suffered death because they proclaimed what they had seen and known.

Today, the mystic is less subject to religious intolerance because public indifference outweighs the shrill hostility of religious bigots, although in its place he is confronted with the derision of an increasingly harsh reductionist materialism. Neither this nor an institutional religion that has become increasingly unsure of its own way forward can feed the human soul that seeks to grow. The mystic can offer a way that does lead to a certain knowledge of God, to an attainment of Divine Union. Not all of us will attain that goal; not all of us will have aspirations that high; but wherever we come to rest on the Mystic Way, we can gain at least a glimpse of the Absolute. It is certainty of this that motivates the mystic in his quest, and that also motivates me in presenting his Way to you.

R.A. Gilbert
Bristol, November 1990

INTRODUCTION

At the end of his life Thomas Aquinas, the great scholastic theologian of the thirteenth century, gave up work on the third and final part of his *Summa Theologica* – the greatest work and most enduring legacy of medieval philosophy – telling his secretary that all his writing had come to an end, because 'all I have written seems to me like so much straw compared with what I have seen and what has been revealed to me.' His thinking and his writing had been the focus of his working life so that whatever he had experienced caused everything else to pale into insignificance. But what was it?

Clearly what had happened to him was both overwhelming and transcendent. It completely changed his way of life – but not his faith – and it could not be described. Neither his state of being nor the Reality that revealed itself was amenable to description by way of everyday language; he could not reveal it to others either by the words of sense experience or through his philosophy. He could only state that something utterly different, something unique had happened to him – and make a value judgement upon it. But what did happen to Aquinas?

The only immediate answer we can give is that he had undergone a mystical experience, but to say that only raises further questions. What does the word 'mystical' mean? What is a mystic? What is the state in which such experiences happen? And, first of all, what *is* mysticism?

Essentially these questions are interdependent. At one level mysticism is simply the study and interpretation – philosophical, psychological and spiritual – of the experiences and behaviour, beliefs, thoughts and speculations of the mystics themselves: those who, like Aquinas, have undergone an overwhelming experience in which they enter an exalted state of consciousness and come face to face with Reality (or whatever they may choose to call it: God, the Absolute, the All in All, or some other collection of superlative terms). More generally mysticism has been given dictionary definitions such as: 'A spiritual discipline aiming at union with the divine through deep meditation or trance-like contemplation', and 'the experience of such communion [i.e. divine union] as described by mystics' (*Readers' Digest Great Illustrated Dictionary*, 1984. This is effectively based on the *Shorter Oxford English Dictionary* with contemporary usages).

While this is far from being an adequate definition it does provide a starting point and avoids interpreting the word in a pejorative sense, as was commonly done by hostile and sceptical critics in the last century (A classic example is that of R.A. Vaughan, for whom 'Mysticism, whether in religion or philosophy, is that form of error which mistakes for a divine manifestation the operations of a merely human faculty' *Hours with the Mystics*, 1856, Vol. 1, p. 26.) Even today the word is all too often loosely used and is treated as synonymous with the irrational, the occult or self delusion in a religious context.

Definitions in specialist works on mysticism or on religious experience in general take us some way forward, but they frequently lack precision and abound in preconceptions which severely restrict our use of the term. Some authors consciously strive to avoid a careful, painstaking definition of the word. Thus Ben-Ami Scharfstein (in *Mystical Experience*, 1973, p. 1) says of it:

Seen very broadly, mysticism is a name for our infinite appetites. Less broadly, it is the assurance that these appetites can be satisfied. Still less broadly, it is some particular attitude towards 'reality' and a view as to how someone or anyone can come into perfect contact with it. And mysticism is also, of course, a name for the paranoid darkness in which unbalanced people stumble so confidently. It is therefore a quality of the life of each of us, beginning with our infinite appetites, continuing with the rise and fall of our hopes that they will be satisfied, and ending with the precarious balance we keep as we stroll, or plod, or stride, or shuffle along the way of sanity, the darkness of self-hatred on one side, and the darkness of self-love on the other.

As a general description of the human condition this account may just pass muster, but as an account of mysticism it will not do. It does, however, reflect what may be called the 'New Age' view of mysticism, a view that skates over the problems involved in attempting to understand the subject. The phenomenon of the mystical experience is not confined to western Christian culture; it is found in all ages and in all religions. The experience may safely be assumed to be the same simply because human beings do not vary in terms of their sense perceptions or their mental processes wherever and whenever they have existed; but their understanding of Reality, their concepts of God, vary dramatically from culture to culture, and while these variations undoubtedly add to the richness of human nature they are yet variations. Where the faiths built upon these varying concepts of God differ in their very essence, contradictions will be found; and where they hold mutually exclusive philosophical and theological doctrines these cannot both be true: one (or possibly both) of the faiths concerned must be false. Of course this does not deny the validity of the underlying Reality, merely the human interpretation put upon it – but it is an abdication of reason to try to pretend that both doctrines can be true. What might be called the 'This is true for you and its contradictory opposite is true for me' syndrome cannot stand up to argument; if we are to make sense of mysticism, to appreciate its value for humanity, and even to talk meaningfully about it, we must, at least, be intellectually honest. Which brings us back to the question of definitions.

I write as a child of western culture, and as my words will be read largely by others whose lives and traditions are rooted in that culture – which, like it or not, is underpinned by the Christian faith and the Judeao-Christian tradition – I will confine myself principally to western definitions of mysticism; the question of mystics in other traditions, their experiences, their writings and their relationship to their own faiths will be considered in later chapters.

The technical definitions of mysticism laid down by philosophers and theologians tend towards either sectarian bias or a confusing linguistic complexity, but as they are found scattered throughout mystical literature we cannot avoid them and, if nothing more, we must cast a cold eye upon them.

Dean Inge,[1] in his famous Bampton Lectures on 'Christian Mysticism' gives – 'only as specimens. The list might be made much longer . . .' – twenty-six definitions of mysticism over fourteen pages of closely printed text. They range from the technicalities of mystical theology to the mind-numbing complexity of nineteenth-century German philosophy, lightened only by Goethe's brief but profound comment that 'Mysticism is the scholastic of the heart, the dialectic of the feelings.' Against this may be set such definitions as 'Mysticism is the filling of the consciousness with a content (feeling, thought, desire), by an involuntary emergence of the same out of the unconscious', and 'The essence of Mysticism is the assertion of an intuition which transcends the temporal categories of the understanding, relying on speculative reason,' or most tortuous of all, 'If the self is not wholly contained in self-consciousness, if man is a being dualised by the threshold of sensibility, then is Mysticism possible; and if the threshold of sensibility is movable, then Mysticism is necessary.' In deference to pious memory I will not identify the authors of this verbiage, but it serves to illustrate the extreme difficulty of discussing non-empirical concepts solely in terms of the intellect.

How, then, can we define mysticism? We may start with its etymology. The word is derived from the Greek mysteries, especially those of Eleusis which were designed to bring the initiate to an awareness of the holy and of the timeless state in which it exists, and for him to gain a secret wisdom which

4

must not be shared with the outside, uninitiated world. For the mundane world the initiate's lips were sealed, and so the word mysterion (mystery) was applied to his experience, deriving from *muein*, to close the eyes or lips. But does this tell us anything about mysticism? It does, for it brings us to the greatest difficulty concerning the subject: the communication of an experience that cannot be described in ordinary language – even if it is permissible to do so.

Thus we are left, or so it would seem, with grandiose definitions that are really rather limp: 'Mysticism is an immediate, intuitive, experimental knowledge of God, . . . it is consciousness of a Beyond, or of transcendent Reality, or of Divine Presence'; 'Mysticism is to possess the infinite in the finite'; 'A study of the supposed essence of religion, or God-consciousness, that prescinds from any particular dogmatic framework.' Better by far is Evelyn Underhill's definition: 'Mysticism is the art of union with Reality. The mystic is a person who has attained that union in a greater or lesser degree; or who aims at and believes in such attainment.' (*Practical Mysticism*, 1914, p. 3) It follows that the knowledge gained from the mystical experience is direct – a direct knowledge of God. Nor is it fancy or speculation; it is true knowledge, albeit knowledge of something quite distinct from the empirical world, and it is important: 'Mysticism', wrote Geoffrey Parrinder (*Mysticism in the World's Religions*, 1976, p. 6), 'is not a plug for gaps as yet unfilled by science but, on the contrary, its conviction of the mystical unity at the heart of things may alone provide that order and continuity upon which all other studies depend.'

And this is something of which the mystic is fully aware. He is, admittedly, seeking to unite his own soul, the core of his being, with the Divine; but this is not a selfish act. Having seen the Divine Vision, or having attained to Divine Union, the mystic does not remain in this exalted state. He comes back, and returns with the burden of duty to his fellow men: the yoke of the Kingdom is upon him. It may be a continuation of his previous labours, a desire to change his life in the service of others (as with St Francis of Assisi), or an overriding need to convey his experiences to others so that they, too, can seek and attain the Divine Union. Or it may be a combination of these, as in the case of Jacob Boehme who wrote his dazzling treatises on mysticism and the mystic state while carrying on his trade as a shoemaker.

Of course not all mystics recorded their experiences and many remain quite unknown, but they yet exercise an influence upon others, who in turn publicize their gifts. Jean-Baptiste Vianney, the Curé d'Ars, brought about a remarkable revival in the spiritual lives not only of his flock but also of many thousands throughout France; his mystical experiences brought out and enhanced his compassion, his innate skill as a spiritual director, and his extraordinary insight into the character of those who came to him. And what he fed to others returned to feed him; his own spiritual life was enriched by the experience of an old peasant of his parish, whom he

> used to see passing long hours of adoration in the church day by day. Astonished at seeing him remain silent, without even moving his lips, the holy curé asked him one day what he used to say to our Lord during those long hours of adoration: 'Oh! I do not say anything,' answered the old man; 'I look at him and he looks at me.'

> (A. Saudreau, *The Mystical State*, 1924, p. 4)

Whether this rapturous adoration involved a true mystical experience we cannot know, but it was certainly a religious experience; that is, a conscious awareness of the Presence of God but not necessarily involving the intense, direct and personal experience of God, the absorption into the Divine that is the hallmark of the mystical experience.

Such religious experiences are far more common than is generally realized. Studies by the Religious Experience Research Unit, set up in Oxford in 1969 by Sir Alister Hardy, have shown that between a third and a half of people questioned in random surveys admit to having been 'aware of, or influenced by a presence or power, whether referred to as God or not, which is different from their "everyday selves"'. The more educated (and thus more articulate) respondents were, the more they were likely to give a positive answer, thus suggesting that the apparent lower incidence of religious experience among the less well-educated was an artefact of literacy, or its lack, as much as of ineffability.

Similarly, Marghanita Laski conducted a survey in 1960 of a small but representative group of people to determine the rarity or otherwise of what she termed the experience of transcendent ecstasy, which may be either secular or religious. The experience proved to be more widespread than she had expected but there was no essentially religious component save where the respondents were already committed to a particular faith. But, centred as they were on the self, these were not technically mystical experiences. There is a clear gradation through these various states of heightened awareness, or altered states of consciousness, which if not commonplace are certainly widespread, to the true mystical state with its essential component of union with the Divine – and what might be called its moral component, the compelling sense of a duty to return to the everyday world and to disseminate a better understanding of the Divine Will and what it demands of that world.

At this point a further problem arises. People may admit to having had religious or ecstatic experiences, and they may recognize some specific event or object that triggered the experience: a piece of music or poetry, or work of art; a personal relationship; a beautiful sunset or landscape. But how can we be sure of the validity of the experience or of the accuracy of their report of it? Indeed, how can the mystic be sure of the validity or specific content of the experience? The manner in which a solution to these problems can be found is considered in a later chapter; here it is enough to be aware of them and to accept the bona fides of the mystic.

For the mystic this problem is more urgent. He returns from the exalted state with a compulsion to communicate his experience to others, but first he must set it in a coherent framework within his own everyday consciousness, for only then can he transmit it to others. Once he has done this, with the inevitable loss of both intensity and detail that committing it to his material memory entails, he must find a way of expressing the experience so that it is comprehensible to others. This task, the communication of the mystical experience, is the most difficult of all for there is, of necessity, no adequate language in which to express what is essentially inexpressible. He must thus make use of such devices as similes, metaphors, and paradox – all accompanied by superlatives, the most powerful words he can find, and with frequent use of sensory images: beyond sense experience though it is there is no other way of describing the mystical experience than by way of the language of sense perception. The sensory image must act as a symbol of that which has no sensory counterpart – 'the deep which gives up no form'.

It might be thought that the task of description is easier for the non-religious mystic – the Nature Mystic as he is often styled – whose exalted experience is inspired by a sense of oneness with the natural world around him. The identification with nature that such mystics feel is not the same as Divine Union and, consequently, the problems of expressing the experience in everyday language are not so great; but ineffability at least justifies the use of similes. For the nature mystic the glory of the setting sun, for example, is simply itself and cannot be used to stand for something beyond sense experience. He must thus describe his experience in terms of the senses involved and of his inner feelings. To avoid triteness in such an account is equally as difficult as for the religious mystic to convey in a meaningful way what he has experienced. Great poets such as Wordsworth can overcome this difficulty, as can lyrical prose writers of the calibre of Richard Jefferies; but for the average man or woman the sense of oneness with nature, if they experience it, will render them inarticulate and it must inevitably remain incommunicable. All they can do is to state that they have had such an experience and liken it, for example, to the feelings expressed by Wordsworth in *Tintern Abbey*:

And I have felt
A presence that disturbs me with the joy
Of elevated thoughts; a sense sublime
Of something far more deeply interfused,
Whose dwelling is the light of setting suns,
And the round ocean, and the living air,
And the blue sky, and in the mind of man:
A motion and a spirit, that impels
All thinking things, all objects of all thought,
And rolls through all things.

Whether or not this is religious mysticism is a contested issue, but it clearly expresses an exaltation of spirit that is far beyond the normal human response to natural beauty. If it does not reflect a mystical state, it is as close an analogue as we are likely to find in ordinary words.

This, then, is mysticism: in brief, the superstructure created by the mystic to convey the nature and meaning of the mystical experience. To understand it more fully, to appreciate its value for us as individuals and for mankind as a whole we must look in depth at the whole range of 'altered states of consciousness' and consider in more detail the differences between the mystical experience and those other experiences that are superficially similar but quite different in essence. We must examine too the various ways in which the mystical experience can be communicated, not only in words but also by non-verbal means. The problem of the psychology of mysticism must also be addressed: what neuro-physiological structures in the brain mediate the mystical experience? how do we know that the mystic is not simply psychologically disturbed? and how do the abnormal and psychic phenomena so often associated with the mystic fit into the framework of healthy mysticism?

Finally, there is the question of the Mystic Way. What exactly must one do to attain the mystic state? For many this will be the most important question, but no consideration of the Mystic Way will make sense until the jumble of other questions has been cleared out of the way. As a necessary foundation for what follows we will look first at the course of mysticism through human history, as it is recorded in the words of the mystics down the ages and in the layers of commentary added – not always for sectarian advantage – by the theologians of all faiths who have come after them. There are no rules governing the exact manner in which these experiences and commentaries must be set out, so it should be noted that the order in which they are presented in the following chapters is simply that which seems appropriate to me.

1 · MYSTICISM IN THE NON-CHRISTIAN WORLD

Louis Claude de Saint-Martin,[1] the 'Unknown Philosopher' once wrote that 'All mystics speak the same language, for they come from the same country', and in so far as there can be only one ultimate Reality, whatever its nature may be, he was correct. But when we look at the work of the philosophers and theologians of mysticism, and at the records of the mystics themselves, we find no unity of expression or even of apparent goal; in attitude, manner and approach they are as diverse as the cultures into which they were born. If they do speak the same language, then it is with very different dialects.

Nor do we know when they first began to speak. There is no reason to suppose that the people of the earliest human cultures could not or did not enter mystical states of a similar nature to those with which we are familiar today, but we cannot say how they interpreted them: how the primitive mystic was treated by his fellows, whether they revered him or reviled him. If we assume (and it must be a cautious assumption) that 'primitive' cultures of the present day preserve the essential features of pre-civilized society, then it is probable that the earliest mystics were treated as beings apart, able to convey the messages of the gods to the people and possessed of supernatural powers – much like the shamans of Siberia (more especially those whose shamanic vocation has been spontaneous, following from visions and ecstasies). These, however, exercise a primarily priestly function and this is not a necessary condition of being a mystic as we now understand the term.

What, then, are our earliest records of mystical experiences displaying the features that we normally associate with them? Egyptian and Babylonian religious records are equivocal as far as mysticism is concerned, and thus we may safely begin with Eleusis, for we have more or less contemporary accounts of the Mysteries[2] as they were in the fifth century BC. Synesius, the Christian Neoplatonist, stated that 'Aristotle is of the opinion that the initiated learned nothing precisely, but that they received impressions and were put into a certain frame of mind.' That the feelings of the initiates, the *mystae*, were profoundly stirred during the Eleusinian ceremonies is clear from Plutarch, who related the spiritual excitement of the mystae to the state of the soul at death:

> When a man dies, he is like those who are being initiated into the Mysteries. The one expression teleutan the other teleisthai correspond . . . [i.e. 'coming to an end' as opposed to achieving fulfilment]. Our whole life is but a succession of wanderings, of painful courses, of long journeys by tortuous ways without outlet. At the moment of quitting it, fears, terrors, quiverings, mortal sweats, and a lethargic stupor, come over us and overwhelm us; but as soon as we are out of it pure spots and meadows receive us, with voices and dances and the solemnities of sacred words and holy sights. It is there that man, having become perfect and initiated – restored to liberty, really master of himself – celebrates crowned with myrtle the most august mysteries, and holds converse with just and pure souls. (Plutarch, *De facie in orbe lunae*: 28, Vol. XII, ed. & trans. H. Chemiss, Loeb edition, 1935)

The Mysteries also differed greatly from what might be called the intellectual mysticism of the Pythagoreans and Neoplatonists: they were positive and life-affirming in a way quite alien to the ethos of Plotinus and his fellows.

This is not to devalue Plotinus: he was the first to set out clearly the idea of the Absolute (the One or the Good in his terms) and the *Enneads*[3] remain one of the world's great classics of metaphysics and mystical philosophy. They also include Plotinus's personal account of his own mystical experiences:

> Many times it has happened: lifted out of the body into myself; becoming external to all other things and self-encentred; beholding a marvellous beauty; then, more than ever, assured of community with the loftiest order; enacting the noblest life, acquiring identity with the divine; stationing within it by having attained that activity; poised above whatsoever within the Intellectual is less than the Supreme: yet, there comes the moment of descent from intellection to reasoning, and after that sojourn in the divine, I ask myself how it happens that I can now be descending, and how did the Soul ever enter into my body, the Soul which, even within the body, is the high thing it has shown itself to be.
>
> (Plotinus, *Ennead* IV.8.1)

In this passage Plotinus describes his experience as if he were an observer of it, making no attempt to express the immediate effect it had upon him, and omitting any reference to the ecstatic components. Much of his work is expository: the bulk of the *Enneads* is devoted to setting out the nature of the Cosmos, and of the Absolute and our relation to it, but he is at pains to insist on the sanctity of the mystical experience. 'This,' he says, 'is the purport of that rule of our Mysteries: "Nothing divulged to the Uninitiate": the Supreme is not to be made a common story, the holy things may not be uncovered to the stranger, to any that has not himself attained to see.' He likens the mystic to one who has 'penetrated the inner sanctuary' and goes on to describe the Divine Vision and the quest for Union.

> There, indeed, it was scarcely vision, unless of a mode unknown; it was a going forth from the self, a simplifying, a renunciation, a reach towards contact and at the same time a repose, a meditation towards adjustment. This is the only seeing of what lies within the holies: to look otherwise is to fail.

But striving to attain these heights is a solitary task. There is no corporate mystical activity for Plotinus:

> This is the life of gods and of the godlike and blessed among men, liberation from the alien that besets us here, a life taking no pleasure in the things of earth, the flight of the alone to the alone.
> (Plotinus, *Ennead* VI.9.11)

Compared with this austere, ascetic and intellectual striving the spiritual work of the Gnostics[4] is crude and unpolished, but there is a raw power in their writings and just as their heavens are vibrant with strange life, so are their personal exaltations filled with passion. In what is among the best known of Gnostic texts, *Pistis Sophia*, the descriptions of the aeons and of their interactions with the soul are put variously in the mouths of Jesus, Sophia herself, Mary and the Disciples. At one point Jesus describes the descent of the light-power upon Sophia:

> Now when these things had happened, the pure light-power within the Sophia began to sing praises; but she sang praises to my light-power which had become a crown on her head. She sang praises, saying thus: 'The light has become a crown on my head and I will not be left without it, so that the emanations of the Authades do not steal it from me.
>
> 'And even if all the materials move, I however will not move. And even if all my materials are destroyed and remain in the Chaos – these which the emanations of the Authades see – I however will not be destroyed.
>
> 'For the light is with me, and I myself am with the light.' But the Pistis Sophia said these words. Now at this time let him who understands the thought of these words come forward and give their interpretation.
> (*Pistis Sophia*, Book I, Chap. 59, trans. Violet Macdermot, 1978)

This Mary and Jesus duly do.

Not all Gnostic texts are as barbarous in their language. The Syrian poem, *The Song of the Pearl*, is a parable of the soul's descent into matter, gradual arousal, and triumphant return to the heavenly Kingdom; while not specifically a mystical text, its language is typical of that used by those who have entered exalted states of being. In these lines the Robe of Glory moves towards the soul:

> Then in its royal movements
>   it was all flowing out towards me,
> And on the hands of its givers
>   it hastened as though I should take it;
> Also me too my love impelled
>   that I should run to meet and welcome it.
> So I stretched out and grasped it,
>   with the beauty of its hues adorned,
> And my mantle of glorious colours
>   I threw it all entirely on.
> I clothed myself therein and soared on high
>   to the Gate of Peace and Adoration.

Analogous to the Gnostic quest for heaven is the Buddhist striving for Nirvana, that paradoxical state so difficult to comprehend. It is not a state of Divine Union for there is no personal God in Buddhism, but it is also not a state of total annihilation of all being, rather is it the extinction of desires. It can be seen as a stillness, the 'unborn and undying eternal state and experience'; but there is no individual consciousness in Nirvana and it is thus quite unlike the goal of western mystics. Most Buddhist mystical texts are concerned with the attainment of Enlightenment, which is, in effect, to enter Nirvana. Gautama Buddha himself described to his disciples his attainment of Nirvana:

> As I knew and perceived this, my mind was freed from desires of the senses, from desire for existence, and from ignorance. As I was liberated knowledge arose that I was liberated. I understood that rebirth was destroyed, that the religious life had been led, that what had to be done was done, and that there was no more for me in this world.
>
> (*Maha-Saccaka Sutta* 1.242)

Mahayana (Great Vehicle) Buddhism, the Buddhism of Tibet, China and Japan, absorbed much from other, older religions and is doctrinally far more complex than its southern counterpart. Many Tibetan texts are both more poetic and more paradoxical than the early Canonical books (the

Sermons of Gautama and contemporary commentaries upon them), but in a curious way this renders them more accessible to western readers despite their difficult language. In *The Jewel Ornament of Liberation* of Sgam.Po.Pa the disciple is guided through a doctrinal maze towards a final and full realization of Buddhahood. If he is usefully to engage in meditative practices he must first understand his own nature – Mind, for example: Mind is neither within nor without,

> Nor is it found anywhere else.
> It is neither mixed with other things, nor apart from them.
> It is not anything whatsoever and therefore
> Beings are by nature in Nirvana.

Instruction, however, is still needed:

> A mind which has found peace through realising that reality has but one emotional value and no differentiating attributes by which one entity is alienated from another, does not abide anywhere and is not attached to anything. This patience (and acceptance of reality) brings great benefit. The strenuousness of the wise consists in giving up all attachment:
>
> > A mind which does not stay anywhere and is attached
> > Is called 'the field of merits'.
> > For the benefit and happiness of all beings
>
> You should practise meditative absorption; take upon yourself this burden and develop a correct view.
> To burn away all conflicting emotions is the sign of the wise.
> (Sgam.Po.Pa., *The Jewel Ornament of Liberation*, trans. & ed.
> H.V. Guenther, 1959, pp. 213 & 222)

But not all Tibetan texts set out the path of spiritual development in terms of this passive contemplation. Ye-she Gyal-Tshan, the tutor of the Eighth Dalai Lama, sets out the 'more secret than secret' path in a poem in *The Secret Manual revealing the Innermost Nature of Seeing Reality*, or *The Source of All Attainments*: (Stanzas 4 to 8).

> May I be favoured by perfection in supreme
> Enlightenment through true compassion when I think
> Of the misery and pain in this great ocean of Being, of
> The beings that are there and are the mother who long sheltered me.

All things within and without like an echo appear
And yet are nothing, they are nothing yet appear.
May I travel this auspicious path quickly to its end, the path on
    which
Appearance and no-thing-ness, fitness of action and intelligence
    unite.

Good and evil in whatever way errancy
May appear are but labels that by my mind are used.
May my mind dwell in the sphere of Reality
And not beneath the spell of hope, fear, lust and hate.

To dire illusions may I not succumb,
But may I with heroes and Dakas dance
In the circle of the lustrous gods and in the joy
Of the music of co-emergent bliss-no-thing-ness.

May I reach soon the citadel of unity
Where inseparable and in embrace most close
Live the young groom called 'The Great Bliss-Awareness'
And 'Reality' the bride immaculate.

(Quoted in: Guenther, H.V. *Treasures on the Tibetan Middle Way*,
1976, p. 134–5)

This sexual imagery has curious parallels, as we shall see, in many Christian mystical texts. The ends are quite different but the way in which the mystical state is depicted by analogy with sexual union is common to both: the physical exaltation that accompanies the sex act is universally understood.

Hindu mystical texts have much in common with those of Buddhism – they were developed in the same cultural milieu – even though their philosophical attitudes are quite distinct. Within Hinduism both Monistic and Theistic texts are found but it is not always easy to determine the stance of a given author. In the case of Sankara[5] it is, however, quite clear: he was the greatest of Indian monistic philosophers and he developed the doctrine of 'a-dvaita' or non-duality which argues that only Brahman is real, all else being illusion and the quest of the (non-real) soul is to become One with Brahman. Such ideas are also expressed in the Upanishads:

The whole universe is Brahman, and one should calmly worship
That as the being in which we live and move and dissolve. . . . It

contains all the world; it never speaks and has no care ... This Soul of mine in the heart is Brahman, and when I go from here I shall merge into it.

(*Chandogya Upanishad*, 3.14)

Sankara sets out the manner of working towards the One, in *Finding the Real Self*:

By resting ever in the Self, the restless mind of him who seeks union is stilled, and all imaginings fade away; therefore make an end of transferring selfhood to things not Self.

Darkness is put away through force and substantial being; force, through substantial being; in the pure, substantial being is not put away; therefore, relying on substantial being, make an end of transferring selfhood to things not Self.

The body of desire is nourished by all new works begun; steadily thinking on this, and effortfully holding desire firm, make an end of transferring selfhood to things not Self. Thinking: 'I am not this separate life but the supreme Eternal', beginning by rejecting all but this, make an end of transferring selfhood to things not Self; it comes from the swift impetus of imaginings.

Understanding the all-selfhood of the Self, by learning, seeking union, entering the Self; it comes from the Self's reflected light in other things.

Neither in taking nor giving does the sage act at all; therefore by ever resting on the One, make an end of transferring selfhood to things not Self.

(Quoted in *Eastern Mysticism* Vol. I Ed. R. Van Over, 1977, p. 175.)

Other Indian mystics are clearly theistic and much of their writing eschews philosophical speculation and doctrinal instruction, concentrating instead on the ever-present reality of God and on its attainment. Such is this poem, *The Wonder of Grace*, from the *Tiru Vasaham* of the ninth-century Manikka Vasahar:

Fool's friend was I, none such may know
   The way of freedom; yet to me
He shew'd the path of love, that so
   Fruit of past deeds might ended be.
Cleansing my mind so foul, He made me like a god.
   Ah who could win that which the Father hath bestowed?

Thinking it right, sin's path I trod.
    But, so that I such paths might leave,
And find His grace, the dancing God,
    Who far beyond our thought doth live.
O wonder passing great! – to me His dancing shewed.
    Ah who could win that which the Father hath bestowed?
(Quoted in *Eastern Mysticism*, Vol I, Ed. R Van Over, 1977, p. 194)

This is clearly experiential but it offers no guide to those who would follow in the poet's footsteps. For that we must turn westward, to the mystics of Islam.

Sufism, which is Islamic mysticism, derives its name from the Arabic word for wool – a reference to the ascetic origin of the early Sufis who wore woollen shirts like those of the Christian hermits whose way of life they sought to emulate. Their doctrines, while not conflicting with Islam, show traces of Christian, Gnostic, Neoplatonic and even Buddhist influences, but their mystical poetry is both original and unique, and whatever it may have taken from other sources is transcended by the genius of the Sufi poets. Their writings are suffused with Love: of God, of man, and of the world, but it is no simple sentimentality. The Sufi Path to God has both seven ascetic 'stages' – repentance, abstinence, renunciation, poverty, patience, trust in God, and satisfaction; and ten spiritual-psychological 'states' – meditation, nearness to God, love, fear, hope, longing, intimacy, tranquility, contemplation and certainty. After passing through these stages and states the Sufi may then, and only then, enter the higher states of mystical consciousness in which Divine union is possible.

According to the old Persian text, the *Kashf al-Mahjub* of Hujwiri: 'There are really two kinds of contemplation. The former is the result of perfect faith, the latter of rapturous love, for in the rapture of love a man attains to such a degree that his whole being is absorbed in the thought of his Beloved and he sees nothing else.' The Sufis also discovered that ecstasy can be obtained through music, dancing and singing, music being a divine influence whose effect would be good or bad according to the spiritual state of the listener. As for dancing, Hujwiri states that, 'When the heart throbs and rapture grows intense, and the agitation of ecstasy in manifested and conventional forms are gone, this is not dancing nor bodily indulgence, but a dissolution of the soul.'

Some Sufi poetry makes much use of hyperbole, but in the context of ecstatic experiences this is excusable. Not that ecstasy is the whole of the mystic's life. The essence of Sufi mysticism is self-renunciation, not a rejection of the world in the manner of extreme ascetics, but a merging of self in the world in order to surrender the heart and to become attuned to God. Then the self is merged in God and the world is viewed as God sees it: full of beauty and peace however noxious it may appear on the surface. As a consequence of this merging of self in God and the world, Sufi poets see God as Absolute Beauty and Absolute Love which are reflected in earthly beauty and earthly love. It is this that leads them to indulge in sensuous imagery that can sometimes be misconstrued; but it is a mysticism of the heart and, fuelled by a constant outpouring of love, Sufi poetry has an exquisite flavour unique to itself.

The ecstatic identification with nature is found in this poem of Jalaluddin Rumi (1207–73):

> I am the dust in the sunlight, I am the ball of the sun,
> To the dust I say: Remain. And to the sun, roll on.
>
> I am the mist of morning. I am the breath of even.
> I am the rustling of the grove, the surging wave of the sea.
>
> I am the mast, the rudder, the steersman and the ship.
> I am the coral reef on which it founders.
>
> I am the tree of life and the parrot in its branches,
> Silence, thought, tongue and voice.
>
> I am the breath of the flute, the spirit of man,
> I am the spark in the stone, the gleam of gold in metal.
>
> The candle and the moth fluttering round it,
> The rose and the nightingale drunk with its fragrance.
>
> I am the chain of being, the circle of the spheres.
> The scale of creation, the rise and the fall.

I am what is and is not. I am – O Thou who knowest,
Jalaluddin, oh, say it – I am the soul in all.

Less elated and less ecstatic is Jami's[6] poem describing the
Creation and the beauty of the created world; but its imagery
is even richer and it perfectly conveys the idea of seeing the
creation through the eyes of God:

From all eternity the Beloved unveiled His beauty in the solitude
of the unseen;

He held up the mirror to His own face, He displayed His loveliness
to Himself.

He was both the spectator and the spectacle; no eye but His had
surveyed the Universe.

All was One, there was no duality, no pretence of 'mine' or 'thine'.

The vast orb of Heaven, with its myriad incomings and outgoings,
was concealed in a single point.

The Creation lay cradled in the sleep of non-existence, like a child
ere it has breathed.

The eye of the Beloved, seeing what was not, regarded nonentity
as existent.

Although He beheld His attributes and qualities as a perfect whole
in His own essence,

Yet He desired that they should be displayed to Him in another
mirror,

And that each one of His eternal attributes should become
manifest accordingly in a diverse form.

Therefore He created the verdant fields of Time and Space and
the life-giving garden of the world,

That every branch and leaf and fruit might show forth His various
perfections.

The cypress gave a hint of His comely stature, the rose gave tidings
of His beauteous countenance.

Wherever Beauty peeped out, Love appeared beside it; wherever
Beauty shone in a rosy cheek, Love lit his torch from that flame.

Wherever Beauty dwelt in dark tresses, Love came and found a
heart entangled in their coils.

Beauty and Love are as body and soul; Beauty is the mine and
Love the precious stone.

They have always been together from the very first; never have
they travelled but in each other's company.

[Quoted in R.A. Nicholson, *The Mystics of Islam*, 1914, pp. 80–81]

In the writings of the Sufi mystics there is a clear fusion – clearer perhaps than is the case with mystics of any other non- or pre-Christian tradition – of the personal experience of the mystic with the theological and philosophical speculations built upon that experience. Whether this is due to the common heritage of Islam, Judaism and Christianity in being all 'Religions of the Book' is unclear, but it is also a western tendency: to add explanation and interpretation to experience. It has never been enough to enter the mystic state and to marvel at it; always the mystic in the west has had work to do – intellectual, moral or spiritual – which is almost certainly related, to a greater or lesser degree, to the concept of salvation that underpins the great religions of the West.

Other traditions of both the past and the present have their mystics and their works have their own undoubted merits, but enough has been given above to illustrate the richness of mystical thought and practice throughout the religions of the world. Now we must turn to the other two of those 'Religions of the Book' and examine the lives and works of the Jewish and Christian mystics. It may seem unjust to set apart Sufi mysticism from that of Judaism and Christianity, given that it is centred on a personal God and not on the remote abstraction that is the Absolute for both Buddhists and Hindus, but there is no saviour figure in Islam to compare with either the potential Messiah of the Jews or Jesus Christ, the actual saviour for Christians, and this is enough – structurally at least: I am not setting any one above another in terms of the inner experience – to justify separating them.

2 · MYSTICISM IN THE WEST

One clear distinction between eastern and western religions is the different emphasis placed upon the individual. This was well expressed by D.T. Suzuki when he wrote, 'Whenever I see a crucified figure of Christ, I cannot help thinking of the gap that lies deep between Christianity and Buddhism. This gap is symbolic of the psychological division separating the East from the West.

'The individual ego asserts itself strongly in the West. In the East, there is no ego, The ego is non-existent and, therefore, there is no ego to be crucified.' (*Mysticism Christian and Buddhist*, 1957, p. 94.)

A further reason for an extended examination of western mystics is the simple matter of their accessibility. The languages in which they thought and wrote translate readily one into another, for having the same cultural roots they embody the same concepts, and their texts are readily available in printed form (as is true now for the great majority of Jewish as well as Christian mystical texts). Their faith also derives from a common source, set out in the collection of books that is the Judaeo-Christian Bible.

Some authors have argued that none of the biblical texts are mystical: notably R. C. Zaehner, who stated unequivocally that 'pre-Christian Judaism is not only unmystical, it is anti-mystical ... exclusively obsessed by the transcendent holiness of God and man's nothingness in face of him' (quoted by Geoffrey Parrinder in *Mysticism in the World's Religions*) and it is true that the transcendence of God (his being utterly above, beyond and independent of the material universe) is stressed more often than is his immanence (his indwelling presence in the world). But the visions of the prophets reflect experiences that are undeniably mystical for all that their purpose is primarily prophetic. This is especially noticeable in Ezekiel's vision: first he sees 'a great cloud, with brightness round about it, and fire flashing forth continually ... and from the midst of it came the likeness of four living creatures.' The creatures constitute a living chariot, for each of them has a wheel beside it and 'the spirit of the living creatures was in the wheels.' But this is no earthly chariot for it bears a celestial throne:

> And above the firmament over their heads there was the likeness of a throne, in appearance like sapphire; and seated above the likeness of a throne was a likeness as it were of a human form. And upward from what had the appearance of his loins I saw as it were gleaming bronze, like the appearance of fire enclosed round about; and downward from what had the appearance of his loins I saw as it were the appearance of fire, and there was brightness round about him. Like the appearance of the bow that is in the cloud on the day of rain, so was the appearance of the brightness round about. Such was the appearance of the likeness of the glory of the Lord.
>
> (Ezekiel 1:26–28)

If we choose to define a mystic as 'one who seeks or attains direct intercourse with God in elevated religious feeling or ecstasy', then the patriarchs who saw and 'walked with God' were undeniably mystics. The poetical books of the Bible also have strong mystical overtones; if we treat the Song of Solomon (or Song of Songs) as allegory rather than as overt erotic poetry then, in terms of its mystical content, it is on a par with the work of the Sufi poets. It begins thus:

> O that you would kiss me with the kisses of your mouth!
> For your love is better than wine,
> your anointing oils are fragrant,
> your name is oil poured out;
> therefore the maidens love you.

But highly charged though this verse is, it need not be taken as sensual imagery. St Bernard of Clairvaux[1] took it as symbolic of the Divine Union; the bridegroom of the poem is the Divine Word and the bride is the soul:

Let Him kiss me with the kisses of His mouth.' Who is it speaks these words? It is the Bride. Who is the Bride? It is the Soul thirsting for God ... She who asks this is held by the bond of love to him from whom she asks it. Of all the sentiments of nature, this of love is the most excellent, especially when it is rendered back to Him who is the principle and fountain of it – that is, God. Nor are there found any expressions equally sweet to signify the mutual affection between the Word of God and the soul, as those of Bridegroom and Bride; inasmuch as between individuals who stand in such relation to each other all things are in common, and they possess nothing separate or divided. They have one inheritance, one dwelling-place, one table, and they are in fact one flesh. If, then, mutual love is especially befitting to a bride and bridegroom, it is not unfitting that the name of Bride is given to a soul which loves.

(St Bernard. *Sermons on the Song of Songs*. VII, quoted in Evelyn Underhill, *Mysticism*, 1930, p. 137–8)

This is, of course, a Christian interpretation, but with allowance for doctrinal language it would not be unexpected among the later Jewish mystics. At the time Judaism as we know it was being formulated, roughly at the beginning of the Christian era, most mystical writings concerned expositions of the Torah, the Law that is enshrined in the pentateuch, the first five books of the Bible. There was in addition much cosmological and metaphysical speculation which has survived in such works as the *Sepher Yetzirah*, or Book of Formation, and the book *Bahir*, and taken together these texts constitute the mystical tradition known as the Kabbalah, that is 'received doctrine' derived from QBL (to receive). It was not, and is not, a fixed and rigid system dependent solely on ancient texts but a living tradition that has seen constant growth and subtle change for almost two thousand years. Its literature is vast and varied, encompassing tortuous analyses of words and verses, complex descriptions of God and of the process of creation, ecstatic descriptions of mystical experience and delightful allegorical stories. The texts that follow have been chosen as typical but they are the minute tip of a vast and hidden iceberg.

First let us look at creation through the mystic's eye, as expressed in the opening verses of the *Sepher Yetzirah*.

1.   In thirty-two mysterious paths of wisdom did the Lord write, the Lord of Hosts, the God of Israel, the Living Elohim, and King of the Universe, the Almighty, Merciful and Gracious God; He is great and exalted and eternally dwelling in the Height, His name is holy, He is exalted and holy. He created His Universe by the three forms of expression: Numbers, Letters and Words.

2.   Ten ineffable Sephiroth[2] and twenty-two basal letters: three mothers, seven double, and twelve simple letters.

3.   Ten ineffable Sephiroth, corresponding to the ten fingers, five over against five and the only token of the convenant in the middle: the word of the tongue and the circumcision of the flesh.

4.   Ten ineffable Sephiroth, ten and not nine, ten and not eleven: understand with wisdom and apprehend with care; examine by means of them and search them out; know, count, and write. Put forth the subject in its light and place the Formator on His throne. He is the only Creator and the only Formator, and no one exists but He: His attributes are ten and have no limits.

5.   The ineffable Sephiroth: their totality is ten; they are, however, without limits: the infinity of the Beginning and the infinity of the End, the infinity of the Good and the infinity of the Evil, the infinity of the Height and the infinity of the Depth, the infinity of the East and the infinity of the West, the infinity of the North and the infinity of the South; and

only one Lord God, the trusty King, rules them all from His holy dwelling in all eternity.

6. Ten ineffable Sephiroth: their appearance is like that of a flash of lightning, their goal is infinite. His word is in them when they emanate and when they return; at His bidding do they haste like a whirlwind; and before His throne do they prostrate themselves.

7. Ten ineffable Sephiroth: their end is in their beginning and likewise their beginning in their end, as the flame is bound to the burning coal. Know, count, and write. The Lord is one and the Formator is one and hath no second beside Him: what number canst thou count before one?

(From *Sepher Yetzirah*, trans. by Knut Stenring, 1923, p. 21–2)

This is cosmological speculation of a wholly different order than that of the rational philosophers; this is speculation using the inner eye and another order of awareness than that of sense-perception. While it does not directly relate the exalted experience of the writer it is derived from such an experience and is fitted to his theological world-view (the stress is always on the Oneness of God, there is an almost obsessive rejection of any form of Gnostic dualism), drawing its imagery of fire and flame from the source of Ezekiel's vision.

It is, however, unlike much later Jewish mysticism in that it does not concern itself directly with exposition of the Torah, such as is found in the *Zohar*, or Book of Splendour, the greatest of all Kabbalistic works and the summit of Jewish mysticism. This collection was not drawn together until the thirteenth century but it is composed of texts which, in their original form, date from some centuries earlier. Throughout its apparently hair-splitting analyses of the Torah runs the thread of ecstasy, a reflection of a direct knowledge of God. This extract is an interpretation of the story of Jacob's journey from Beer-sheba to Haran (Genesis 28:10):

Inside the hidden nexus, from within the sealed secret, a splendour flashed, shining as a mirror, embracing two colours blended together. Once these two absorbed each other, all colours appeared: purple, the whole spectrum of colours, flashing, disappearing. Those rays of colour do not wait to be seen; they merge into the fusion of splendour.

In this splendour dwells the one who dwells. It provides a name for the one who is concealed and totally unknown. It is called the Voice of Jacob. Complete faith in the one who is concealed and totally unknown belongs here. Here dwells YHVH, perfection of all sides, above and below. Here Jacob is found, perfection of the patriarchs, linked to all sides. This splendour is called by the singled-out name: 'Jacob, whom I have chosen' (Isaiah 41:8). Two names he is called: Jacob and Israel. At first Jacob; later, Israel.

The secret of this secret: First he attained the End of Thought, the elucidation of the Written Torah. She is the Oral Torah, called Be'er, as it is said: 'Moses began be'er, to explain, the Torah' (Deuteronomy 1:5). She is a be'er, a well and an explanation of the one who is called Sheba, Seven, as it is written: 'It took him sheba, seven, years to build it' (I Kings 6:38). Sheba is the Mighty Voice, while the End of Thought is Be'er Sheba.

(From the *Zohar*, trans. by D. Chanan Matt, 1983 p. 75–76)

It is the great achievement of Kabbalism to have taken up the dry formalism of Talmudic exposition and to have infused it with the fervour that stems from the mystical experience. And despite centuries of persecution, Jewish mystics maintained their fervour and their piety; sometimes – as with the mysticism deriving from the work of Isaac Luria in the sixteenth century – it is marked with language that strives too hard to express the inexpressible and all sensible meaning is all but lost beneath the exotic imagery, while in the frenzy surrounding the seventeenth century pseudo-Messiah Sabbatai Zevi, almost all rational meaning is lost and the underlying experience remains forever buried in the text and hidden from the reader. But in the heart of the Enlightenment a great revival of Jewish mysticism occurred with the appearance of the Hasidim in Eastern Europe. This mystical, revivalist movement began with the Baalshem, a simple but wise man whose doctrines were taught by his followers by way of legends about his life and experiences; the Hasidim practised a joyous, ecstatic form of religion expressed outwardly in song and dance, yet remaining firmly entrenched within the essential beliefs and practices of Judaism. The following extracts from Martin Buber's retelling of Hasidic doctrines and stories convey its flavour:

Aboda, or Service

Hitlahabut is the ecstasy of the divine, beyond time or space. Hitlahabut is the mystic meal. Aboda is the service of God in time and space.

Between these two poles the life of the saints oscillates. Hitlahabut is silent, for it lies in the heart of God. Aboda asks: 'What am I and what is my life, so that I may offer up my blood and ardour to thee?'

All is God, and all serves God. This is the primeval duality, a duality developed in the life of the saints, and folded up in the being of the world.

This is the mystery from which a man is kept at a distance if he speaks of it, but which lives in the breast of the souls who seek after and possess God. Known in their longing, slumbering in germ in their ecstasy, and linked up in the rhythm of their actions.

Hitlahabut is as far from Aboda as is fulfilment from longing, and yet it streams out of Aboda as does the finding of God out of the seeking after God.

(Martin Buber, *Jewish Mysticism and the Legends of Baalshem*, 1931, p. 9)

Kavana, or Intention

Kavana is the mystery of a soul, which is concentrated on a single aim, but it is not will. It has no idea of transferring an image of the mind into the world of actual things, nor of materialising a dream into an object, which can be perceived at pleasure again and again. . . . Kavana is a ray of God's glory, dwelling in all men, and signifying redemption.

It is redemption that the Shekinah [i.e. the Glory of God, not conceived as a feminine aspect of God but invariably portrayed in female form] should return from exile, that all the husks should fall from the 'Splendour of God', which should purify itself and become one and unite with its Lord in complete unity. 'In witness of this the Messiah will appear and set all existence free.' It seems to many a one all his life long as though this must happen here and now. For he hears the voices of that which is to be howling in the defiles, and he feels a germinating of eternity in the fields of time, even as though it were in his own blood, and thus he can never think otherwise but that this and this are the appointed moment, and his longing urges him ever the more hotly, for the voices speak ever more commandingly and the germs swell more and more urgently. It is said of one Zaddik [i.e. the righteous, the holy man] that such was his expectation of redemption, that if he heard a tumult in the street he was at once moved to ask what this meant, and whether a messenger had not arrived; and always when he went to sleep he told his servant that he must awake him the moment the messenger had come.

For the coming of the Deliverer was as fixed in his mind as when a father expects his only son from a strange country, and stands on the watch-tower with longing in his eyes, and peers through every window, and, if the door is opened, hastens out to see if his son is not yet come.

(Martin Buber, *Jewish Mysticism and the Legends of Baalshem*, 1931, p. 19–20.)

Buber brought Hasidic mysticism into the present day through the medium of his book *I and Thou* (1937) in which he sets out the nature of God as it relates to the mystic's consciousness: 'The one primary word is the combination I-Thou. The other primary word is the combination I-It'; and knowledge of God consists in meeting him both in the world and beyond it:

Of course God is the 'wholly other'; but He is also the wholly Same, the wholly present. Of course He is the Mysterium Tremendum that appears and overthrows; but He is also the mystery of the self-evident, nearer to me than my I.

Not only in this but throughout all Jewish mysticism there is the essential desire for Union with God; nowhere is there the sense of man's identity with the Divine. God is creator and sustainer of the universe and Man is part of God's creation – he is quite definitely not a part of God himself. And this 'otherness' of God is precisely what is found in Christian mysticism; God is necessarily both transcendent and immanent at the same time, but man's ultimate goal is Divine Union, not cessation of being.

Christian mysticism finds its earliest expression in St Paul's letters. Writing to the Corinthians, he says:

> I must boast; there is nothing to be gained by it, but I will go on to visions and revelations from the Lord. I know a man in Christ who fourteen years ago was caught up to the third heaven – whether in the body or out of the body I do not know, God knows. And I know that this man was caught up into paradise – whether in the body or out of the body I do not know, God knows – and he heard things that cannot be told, which man may not utter.
>
> (2 Corinthians 12:1–4)

This experience was sacred: he does not say that he was unable to speak of it but that he was not allowed to speak. Not all mystics have felt the same constraint; for many an essential part of their experiences has been the urgent need to give out their essence to the world.

The earliest Christian mystical writers did treat these mysteries as something to be kept apart, but they did not construct a systematic mystical theology – that came about only with the work of the Syrian theologian who, in the fifth century, wrote under the name of Dionysius the Areopagite. For him the object of the mystic's quest for union is the Darkness of Unknowing, the Divine Darkness that he wrestles to describe:

> Unto this Darkness which is beyond Light we pray that we may come, and may attain unto vision through the loss of sight and knowledge, and that in ceasing thus to see or to know we may learn to know that which is beyond all perception and understanding (for this emptying of our faculties is true sight and knowledge), and that we may offer Him that transcends all things the praises of a transcendent hymnody, which we shall do by denying or removing all things that are – like as men who, carving a statue out of marble, remove all the impediments that hinder the clear perceptive of the latent image and by this mere removal display the hidden statue itself in its hidden beauty. Now we must wholly distinguish this negative method from that of positive statements. For when we were making positive statements we began with the most universal statements, and then through intermediate terms we came at last to particular titles, but now ascending upwards from particular to universal

conceptions we strip off all qualities in order that we may attain a naked knowledge of that Unknowing which in all existent things is enwrapped by all objects of knowledge, and that we may begin to see that super-essential Darkness which is hidden by all the light that is in existent things.

(*The Mystical Theology*, Chapter 2; trans. by C.E. Rolt, 1920)

This way of understanding, that of stripping away all attributes until one arrives at undifferentiated Being, has remained the preferred way of mystical theologians of the Eastern Churches (although not necessarily of the mystics themselves, who have often strayed from the orthodox path in their pursuit of Reality and in their desire to express it in a meaningful way). Dionysius is at pains to stress that we have no means of describing the Absolute:

It transcends all affirmation by being the perfect and unique Cause of all things, and transcends all negation by the pre-eminence of Its simple and absolute nature – free from every limitation and beyond them all.

(*The Mystical Theology*, Chapters 1 and 5; trans. by C.E. Rolt, 1920)

But for the mystic, experience of the Divine is certain. A century before Dionysius was writing, St Augustine[3] described his experience of the Divine Vision:

And when this power also within me found itself changeable, it lifted itself up to its own intelligence, and withdrew its thoughts from experience, abstracting itself from the contradictory throng of sensuous images, that it might find out what that light was wherein it was bathed, when it cried out that beyond doubt the unchangeable was better than the changeable, and how it came to know the unchangeable, which it must have known in some way or another, for otherwise it could not have preferred it so confidently to the changeable. And thus, with the flash of one hurried glance, it attained to the vision of THAT WHICH IS. And then at last I saw Thy invisible things understood by means of the things that are made, but I could not sustain my gaze; my weakness was dashed back, and I was relegated to my ordinary experience, bearing with me nothing but a loving remembrance, cherishing, as it were, the fragrance of those viands which I was not yet able to feed upon.

(St Augustine, *Confessions*, Chapter 17; trans. by C. Bigg, 1898)

This sudden vision – an analogue, perhaps, of the Buddhist experience of 'sudden enlightenment' – did not preclude union with the Divine. Elsewhere Augustine tells of a direct experience that went beyond vision; in it he is emphasizing, as do many other mystics, the timelessness of the Divine presence:

> And so we came to our own minds, and passed beyond them into the region of unfailing plenty, where Thou feedest Israel for ever with the food of truth, where Life is Wisdom by which all these things come to be, but is, as it was, and shall be evermore, because in it is neither past nor future but present only, for it is eternal; for past and future are not eternal. And as we talked and yearned after it, we touched it for an instant with the whole force of our hearts. And we sighed, and left there impawned the first-fruits of the spirit, and heard again the babble of our own tongues, wherein each word has a beginning and ending. Far unlike Thy Word, our Lord, who abides in Himself, never growing old and making all things new.
>
> (*Confessions*, Chapter 10)

There is such a wealth of Christian mystical texts, and so many are readily available in print, that it would serve no useful purpose to provide an endless anthology of selected texts. However, to understand the varieties of mystical experience as they have been recorded in the West, it is essential to quote from the works of the more luminous of those mystics who represent different approaches to the quest for, and attainment of, Divine Union. Choosing these is necessarily a highly personal affair, and it must not be supposed that I am passing value judgments upon those mystics – the great majority – whom I neither quote from nor mention, but equally it is not the case that those selected are in any way unrepresentative; they are chosen to illustrate specific points and are not in any way either better or worse; more or less holy; more sane or more unbalanced than any of their fellows (and, should the last point evoke surprise, I would add that the more unbalanced ecstatics and visionaries I do not accept – as we shall see – as mystics in the true sense of the word.)

In England there was during the fourteenth century, for various reasons, social as well as religious, an upsurge in religious vocations – with a consequent increase in devotional and mystical literature. Some of this was of a very high spiritual order, and the best of it is justly placed among the greatest of mystical writing that the world has seen. One text is anonymous, its unknown author modelling himself on pseudo-Dionysius, but taking no name at all; he is thus known to us only through his classic text, *The Cloud of Unknowing*. In this he advises the would-be mystic to persist in his efforts to pass through this cloud, which is no material thing but, 'when I say darkness, I mean a lacking of knowing: as all things that thou knowest not, or hast forgotten, is dark to thee; for thou seest it not with thy ghostly eye. And for this reason it is called, not a cloud of the air, but a cloud of unknowing; which is betwixt thee and thy God.' It can, however, be penetrated if one has 'in thy will a naked intent unto God', but it will not be a direct vision, for 'if ever thou shalt see Him or feel Him, as it may be here, it must always be in this cloud, and in this darkness. And if thou wilt busily travail as I bid thee, I trust in His mercy that thou shalt come thereto.'

The author of the *Cloud of Unknowing* is also eminently practical and instructs his readers in the way they may achieve this being 'Oned with God'; it is through the practice of the contemplative life, achieved by rising from the active life – 'good and honest bodily works of mercy and of charity' – through the mixed life in which active works and contemplation overlap in contrition, compassion for the misery of others, worship and pious meditation, to the true contemplative life which 'hangeth all wholly in this darkness and in this cloud of unknowing, with a loving stirring and a blind beholding unto the naked being of God Himself only.' The power that enables this life to be lived is not reason, but love; all rational creatures have two 'working powers', the one being called a knowing power and the other, a loving power:

Of the which two powers, to the first, God who is the maker of them is evermore incomprehensible; but to the second, He is, in every man diversely, all comprehensible to the full. Insomuch that one loving soul alone in itself, by virtue of love, may comprehend in itself Him who is sufficient to the full – and much more, without comparison – to fill all the souls and angels that may be. And this is the endless marvellous miracle of love.

(*The Cloud of Unknowing*, ed. Dom Justin McCann, 1924, p. 7)

Love can aid in driving out sin from the soul: 'for this only by itself is that work that destroyeth the ground and root of sin.' And it is love alone, not thought, that enables one to approach God:

Of God Himself can no man think. And therefore I would leave all that thing that I can think, and choose to my love that thing that I cannot think. For why, He may well be loved, but not thought. By love may he be gotten and holden; but by thought never.

At the peak of the contemplative's attainment God may respond and move towards him:

Then will He sometimes peradventure send out a beam of ghostly light, piercing this cloud of unknowing that is betwixt thee and Him, and show thee some of his secrets, the which man may not and cannot speak. Then shalt thou feel thine affection inflamed with the fire of His love, far more than I can tell thee, or may or will at this time. For of that work that pertaineth only to God dare I not take upon me to speak with my blabbering fleshly tongue: and, shortly to say, although I durst I would not.

(*The Cloud of Unknowing*, p. 39)

There is far more in this most perceptive of mystics on the pitfalls of the Way; the behaviour of pseudo-mystics; and the value of the mystic's work to all mankind. We shall return to him more than once, but we must look also at one of his contemporaries, the Lady Julian of Norwich whose *Revelations of Divine Love* came to her during her life as an ascetic religious solitary (an Anchoress). She recorded her experiences in great detail and after twenty years of disciplined thinking, praying and meditating about them, she gave them out to the world – to her 'even-Christians'. Her work begins with her visions and ends with her insights upon them; at first, she says, 'our Lord shewed me a spiritual sight of His homely loving' and then,

> Also in this He shewed me a little thing, the quantity of an hazel-nut, in the palm of my hand; and it was as round as a ball. I looked thereupon with eye of my understanding, and thought: What may this be? And it was answered generally thus: It is all that is made. I marvelled how it might last, for methought it might suddenly have fallen to naught for littleness. And I was answered in my understanding: It lasteth, and ever shall last for that God loveth it. And so all-things hath the Being by the love of God.
>
> (Julian of Norwich, *Revelations of Divine Love*, ed. by Grace Warrack, 1901, p. 10)

Her fifteen revelations were accompanied by her own bodily illness and she dwells in a manner that may seem unhealthy to the modern reader on the physical aspects of Christ's passion; but she was well aware of the mental and spiritual pitfalls into which her illness could lead her and she distinguished clearly between what she saw in dreams and her spiritual revelations. She concludes her work with an explanation of God's purpose in bringing her these experiences:

> And from that time that it was shewed I desired oftentimes to learn what was our Lord's meaning. And fifteen years after, and more, I was answered in ghostly understanding, saying thus: Wouldst thou learn thy Lord's meaning in this thing? Learn it well: Love was His meaning. Who shewed it thee? Love. What shewed He thee? Love. Wherefore shewed it thee? For Love. Hold thee therein and thou shalt learn and know more in the same. But thou shalt never know nor learn therein other thing without end. Thus was I learned that Love was our Lord's meaning.
>
> And I saw full surely that ere God made us He loved us; which love was never slacked, nor ever shall be. And in this love He hath done all His works; and in this love He hath made all things profitable to us; and in this love our life is everlasting.

> In our making we had beginning; but the love wherein He made
> us was in Him from without beginning: in which love we have
> our beginning. And all this shall we see in God, without end.
>
> (*Revelations of Divine Love*, p. 10)

Thus for Julian her work was Divine Love poured first into her and then through her into the world by way of her writing. There is little of metaphysical speculation following upon her experiences and in this she contrasts sharply with the continental mystics of her day. They, too, were concerned with Divine Love but their intellectual analyses and expositions developed a mystical theology that bordered (in the eyes of the Church) on heresy. Especially was this so in the case of the greatest of all of them: Meister Eckhart.

As a Dominican friar Eckhart's principal duty was to preach, and it is chiefly in his sermons that his mystical doctrines are expounded. But his influence in Germany and throughout Europe at the beginning of the fourteenth century stemmed as much from his skill as an administrator, teacher and theologian as from the eloquence and power of his preaching, although it was the content of his sermons and other writings that led to charges of heresy (specifically pantheism) being laid against him. At the end of his life Eckhart officially recanted these supposed heresies but they are in effect problems of language rather than of doctrine. His contemporaries lacked the mental agility to understand what he was trying to do: to express the ineffable nature of God in language appropriate to both laymen (and women – many of his sermons were preached to congregations of nuns) and theologians. Above all his words illustrate the extreme difficulty of conveying the mystical experience to others and of constructing an institutionally acceptable theological and philosophical world-view into which it will fit.

He was prepared to admit to error, but not to heresy; his accusers, he said, 'regard as error whatever they fail to understand and also regard all error as heresy, whereas only obstinate addiction to error constitutes both heresy and the heretic.' But what did Eckhart say? Was it pantheism that he taught? Let us see.

Typical of the sermons that caused anxiety to minds less

agile than Eckhart's was one on Ephesians 4:23 'You shall be renewed in the spirit of your mind'. It includes the following passages:

> Now observe: God is nameless because none can say or understand anything about Him. Concerning this a pagan master says that what we understand or declare about the first cause is more what we ourselves are than what the first cause is, because it is above all speech or understanding. If I now say God is good, it is not true; rather, I am good, God is not good. I will go further and say I am better than God: for what is good can become better, and what can become better can become best of all. Now God is not good, therefore he cannot become better. And since he cannot become better, therefore he cannot become best; for these three, good, better and best, are remote from God, since He is above them all. Thus, too, if I say God is wise, it is not true: I am wiser than He. So too if I say God is a being, that is not true: He is a transcendent being, and a superessential nothingness. ... Nor should you seek to understand anything about God, for God is above all understanding. One master [i.e. Augustine] says 'If I had a God I could understand, I would no longer consider him God.' ... 'Oh, but what should I do then?' You should wholly sink away from your youness and dissolve into His Hisness, and your 'yours' and His 'His' should become so completely one 'Mine' that with Him you understand his unbecome Isness and His nameless Nothingness.
>
> ... But if I am to know God without means, then I must really become He and He I. I say further: God must really become I and I must really become God, so fully one that this 'he' and 'I' become and are one 'is', and in that 'isness' work one work eternally, for this 'he' and this 'I' – that is, God and the soul – are very fruitful.

Eckhart's imaginary questioner then asks how God should be loved:

> You should love Him as He is: a non-God, a non-spirit, a non-person, a non-image; rather, as He is a sheer pure limpid One, detached from all duality.
>
> And in that One may we eternally sink from nothingness to nothingness. So help us God. Amen.
>
> (Meister Eckhart, *Sermons and Treatises*, Vol II; trans. by M.O'C. Walshe, 1979, p. 333–335.)

This language, as with that of Eckhart's other sermons touching on the nature of God, is difficult in the extreme. Nor does he help matters by not providing rules for contemplation or a guide to the mystic Way; but he does say that the way to follow is that of the passive mind. Here he is speaking of the Father giving birth to the Son 'in the ground and essence of the soul' so that He 'unites Himself with her':

'Is it better to do something towards this, to imagine and think about God?' asks the questioner, 'or should he keep still and silent in peace and quiet and let God speak and work in him, merely waiting for God to act?' This may be well for 'good and perfected people', but for the rest, 'They must know that the very best and noblest attainment in this life is to be silent and let God work and speak within. When the powers [i.e. the processes through which the soul operates: memory, will, intellect, anger, desire and the senses] have been completely withdrawn from all their works and images, then the Word is spoken. Therefore he said: 'In the midst of the silence the secret word was spoken unto me. (Meister Eckhart, *Sermons and Treatises*, Sermon One, trans. by M.O'C. Walshe, 1979, p. 6–7)

Intellectual mysticism of this kind, and the mystical philosophy built upon it, may appeal to speculative thinkers today but it held little attraction for the pious of Eckhart's day. What they required was the fervent devotion of a Julian of Norwich, or of the Beguines of the Low Countries: they needed a mysticism of the heart which could not sit easily with the scholastic philosophy that still held sway in the declining Middle Ages. But a new era would soon sweep away old modes of thought and make room for a new type of mystic, one who spoke more directly to the heart – and it is these new mystics who speak even more clearly to us who have come after them.

3 · THE REBIRTH OF MYSTICISM

The cultural phenomenon that we call the Renaissance was more than a rebirth of classical learning: it heralded also a revivifying of religion that would lead to both religious and political upheaval in the sixteenth century, to the ferment of Reformation and Counter-Reformation, and to a renewal of the spiritual life on both sides of the new religious divide. It was, however, in Catholic Spain that the greatest flowering of mysticism occurred, more particularly in the persons of St Teresa of Avila (1515–82) and St John of the Cross (1542–91).

Their names are essentially linked not only through their writings but also through their joint labours in reforming and expanding the Carmelite Order. They both wrote for the benefit of those committed to the religious life, but their works are timeless and Professor Allison Peers's comments on Teresa could be applied to either of them: 'The works of St Teresa are a legacy to all who call themselves or would fain be called mystics in spirit and in truth, and as such they have never lacked a multitude of readers.' (*Spanish Mysticism*, 1924, p. 99)

Teresa was unquestionably a passionate mystic, given to vivid imagery and often extravagant language; but her writing is powerful and effective whether she is describing her visions, offering instruction in the four degrees of prayer, or – as in this extract from her *Life* – recounting her experience of the mystical state; she had been unwell and was not seeking any form of exaltation, but 'there came to me a spiritual impulse of such vehemence that resistance to it was impossible. I thought I was being carried up to Heaven.' She feared delusion but was reassured by her confessor, and so,

> With the progress of time, the Lord continued to show me further great secrets: sometimes He does so still. The soul may wish to see more than is pictured to it, but there is no way in which it may do so, nor is it possible that it should; and so I never on any occasion saw more than the Lord was pleased to show me. What I saw was so great that the smallest part of it was sufficient to leave my soul amazed and to do it so much good that it esteemed and considered all the things of this life as of little worth. I wish I could give a description of at least the smallest part of what I learned, but, when I try to discover a way of doing so, I find it impossible; for, while the light we see here and that other light are both light, there is no comparison between the two and the brightness of the sun seems quite dull if compared with the other. In short, however skilful the imagination may be, it will not succeed in picturing or describing what that light is like, nor a single one of those things which I learned from the Lord with a joy so sovereign as to be indescribable. For all the senses rejoice in a high degree, and with a sweetness impossible to describe, for which reason it is better to say no more about it.
>
> (*Life*, Chapter 38, trans. by E. Allison Peers, 1946.)

This is far more effective in conveying the nature of the mystical experience than is Eckhart's wrestling with words to find a theological description of the encounter with God. Teresa also provided detailed instructions for the four stages of mental prayer that lead to the ecstasy of Divine Union, and the clarity with which these are set out provides a strong argument for her mental stability – which has been called in question by some who would see her ecstasies as nothing more than signs of sexual repression. In fact she typifies the essential normality of the mystic, for the sound common sense and administrative zeal with which she carried out the Carmelite reforms would have been beyond the capacity of an unbalanced hysteric – as would the sheer bulk of her correspondence: the letters that reveal her as a busy, methodical and practical woman of affairs.

When we turn to St John of the Cross, however, matters are somewhat different. The chosen hardships of an ascetic life were compounded by the rigours of imprisonment (he was held for a time by the unreformed Carmelites) but he proved to be an inspired spiritual director – Teresa would write of him that 'I have not found another like him in the whole of Castile, nor any that inspires such fervour in those that tread the way to Heaven' – and during the 1580s he composed a remarkable body of mystical poetry, and the prose works that are commentaries on the poems.

As with St Teresa, the writings of St John of the Cross have the virtue of accessibility, with the added bonus that the poems are exquisite works of art. Prefixed to *The Ascent of Mount Carmel* and *The Dark Night of the Soul* are the eight stanzas that make up his best-known poem, and which those texts analyse and interpret. The purpose of these lines is made quite clear in a long subtitle: 'Wherein the soul sings of the happy chance which it had in passing through the dark night of faith, in detachment and purgation of itself, to union with the Beloved.' The stanzas themselves are reminiscent of the Song of Solomon and illustrate one of the ways in which ecstasy can be expressed:

On a dark night, Kindled in love with yearnings – oh, happy chance! –
I went forth without being observed, My house being now at rest.

In darkness and secure, By the secret ladder, disguised – oh, happy chance! –
In darkness and concealment, My house being now at rest.

In the happy night, In secret, when none saw me, Nor I beheld aught,
Without light or guide, save that which burned in my heart.

This light guided me More surely than the light of noonday,
To the place where he (I well knew who!) was awaiting me –

A place where none appeared.

Oh, night that guided me, Oh night more lovely than the dawn,
Oh, night that joined Beloved with lover, Lover transformed in the
  Beloved!

Upon my flowery breast, Kept wholly for himself alone, There
  he stayed sleeping, and I caressed him, And the fanning of the
  cedars made a breeze.

The breeze blew from the turret As I parted his locks;
  With his gentle hand he wounded my neck And caused all my
  senses to be suspended.

I remained, lost in oblivion; My face I reclined on the Beloved.
All ceased and I abandoned myself, Leaving my cares forgotten
  among the lilies.

(St John of the Cross, *Complete Works*, trans. by E. Allison Peers,
1953)

In fact, the *Ascent of Mount Carmel* and the *Dark Night of the Soul* together act as commentaries only on the first three stanzas so that the other five must stand alone for each reader to take up and understand. St John gives his general interpretation at the beginning of the *Ascent*:

The first night or purgation is of the sensual part of the soul, . . .
And the second is of the spiritual part; . . .

  And this first night pertains to beginners, occurring at the time
when God begins to bring them into the state of contemplation;
in this night the spirit likewise has a part, as we shall say in
due course. And the second night, or purification, pertains to
those who are already proficient, occurring at the time when
God desires to bring them to the state of union with God. And
this latter night is a more obscure and dark and terrible purgation,
as we shall say afterwards.

[(St John of the Cross, *Complete Works*)

Put in other words, the first is the Night of Sense and the second is the Night of the Spirit, and they can be seen as analogues of the Divine Vision and the Divine Union, although as St John uses it, the first Night is not of such a high order as this. He differs from the more philosophical mystics in that he suggests both active and passive ways of entering into the mystical life, but ultimate attainment of the true unitive state does depend on a life of utter detachment: it is a dark, difficult and solitary path. Even so, as with all true mystics it is a path of Love.

Divine Union – the final goal of the mystic – was seen as the purpose of the spiritual life by Protestants as well as Catholics, but for reasons that are unclear (but probably to do with cultural milieu) the Protestant mystics do not tend towards emotive speech, preferring the dry language of theology, however odd their usage might be. Their experiences, however, mirror those of the Catholic mystics as can be seen in one of the accounts of Jacob Boehme (1525–1624), the German mystic, of his successful striving after God:

> When I plainly found out that good and evil are in all things, as well in the elements as in creatures; and that in this world the God-fearing fare no better than the Godless, I fell into depression and sadness, and not even the Scriptures, which were well known to me, could give me any comfort. The devil must surely have rejoiced at this, and often impressed my mind with heathenish thoughts, whereof I will make no mention here. . . . But as, in my awakened zeal and eagerness, I stormed violently against God and all the Gates of Hell, . . . my spirit at last broke through into the innermost Birth of the Divinity and was caught up in Love, as a Bridegroom embraces his dear Bride. The triumph in my soul cannot be told or described; I can liken it only to the birth of life through death, and compare it to a resurrection from the dead.
>
> (Jacob Boehme, *Aurora*, Chapter 19, 8–12, Eng trans. ed. by C.J. Barker, 1910)

As a direct consequence of this overwhelming experience (which took place in 1600) Boehme felt a oneness with nature which determined his life's work:

> In this light my spirit suddenly saw through all, and in and by all creatures, even in herbs and grass it knew God, who he is, and how he is, and what his will is: And suddenly in that light my will was set on by a mighty impulse, to describe the being of God.

Elsewhere the poor shoemaker of Goerlitz related this second experience at greater length:

In this my most earnest seeking and desire, ... a gate was opened unto me, so that in a quarter of an hour, I saw and learnt more than if I had studied many years in some university; ... for I perceived and recognised the Being of all beings, the Byss and the Abyss; also the birth of the Holy Trinity, the descent and origin of this world and of all creatures, through the Divine Wisdom. I discovered also within myself the three worlds, namely: 1. the divine, angelical or paradisical; then 2. the dark world, as the original of nature to the fire; and of 3. this external visible world, as a procreation or external birth, or as a substance manifested forth out of both inner and spiritual worlds. I saw and understood the whole nature of good and evil, their origin and mutual relation, and what constitutes the womb of the genetrix; so that I not only wondered greatly, but also rejoiced.

And it was powerfully borne upon my mind to write down these things as a Memorial, however difficult they might be of apprehension to my outer self, and of expression through my pen. I felt compelled to begin at once like a child going to school, to work upon this very great Mystery. Interiorly I saw it all well enough, as in a great depth; for I looked through as into a chaos wherein all things lie; but the unravelling thereof proved impossible.

(Jacob Boehme, *Epistle* 2, trans. ed. by C.J. Barker, 1910)

Or almost impossible. For the last twelve years of his life (he died in 1624) Boehme struggled to unravel the nature of God and the universe: 'whatsoever I could grasp sufficiently to bring it out, that I wrote down.' In more than thirty books he set out his doctrines – a strange mixture of alchemical and kabbalistic symbolism, Lutheran theology and concepts derived from German 'Spiritual Reformers' who had been propagating theosophical and hermetic ideas for fifty years and more. As had many mystics before him, Boehme tried to balance his experiences and his interpretation of them with the orthodoxy of the time; like Eckhart he failed and he was actively, if intermittently, persecuted by his Lutheran parish priest. His works are exasperating; again and again one seems to be on the brink of understanding only to be whirled away into the depths of incomprehension. But Boehme is of signal importance for he represents a turning point in the progress of mystical experience throughout human history.

As the seventeenth century drew on, institutional mysticism declined as religious vocations dwindled and religious observance decayed into religiosity. There are, indeed, many hundreds of devotional and spiritual writers of all denominations who are labelled 'mystics', but for most of them it is an unearned title. Throughout the modern era the mantle of the mystic has fallen for the most part on to the shoulders of what may be termed 'religious amateurs': poets, artists, enthusiasts of doubtful orthodoxy, and avowedly hermetic writers; and there are others who, while they reject any traditional religious faith, are unquestionably mystics in the true mould. How all of these differ from the religious mystics of the past and how they relate to those who seek the mystic Way today, we must now consider. But to do justice to those who are still called to the religious life – and to bring this sample of Christian mystics to ten: 'ten and not nine, ten and not eleven' as with the 'Ten ineffable Sephiroth' – we may look at one from this century.

The Jesuit scholar Teilhard de Chardin (1881–1955) is known for the works of genius in which he fused the processes of biological evolution with the intrusion of Christ into creation. By raising evolution to the spiritual realm he brought the theologian and scientist together after a century of war between reactionary religion and blind materialism; but he was also a profound philosopher of mysticism (he was, by his own admission, 'not qualified' to describe the highest mystical states and would have rejected the label of 'mystic' applied to himself). In his essay 'The Mystical Milieu' he suggests five 'Circles' – analogous to the stages of St Teresa's 'Interior Castle' – through which the mystic travels, being those of presence, consistence, energy, spirit and person. His conclusion deserves notice:

> Moreover, from the humblest dawn of mystical thought, God is seen to be the only being that can maintain and direct it. Although, no doubt, we can by artificial means find some ways of briefly stimulating it, the zest for life, which is the source of all passion and all insight, even divine, does not come to us from ourselves. We are incapable of modifying those primordial

depths of ourselves from which springs the force that animates us. All we can do is to accept ourselves as we are. It is God who has to give us *the impulse of wanting him*. And when the soul feels itself on fire for heaven, it still cannot, by itself, see what it lacks. It will see God only if God turns his face towards it: and a man cannot even force another man to do that. And when, finally, the soul has distinguished the burning centre which has been seeking for it, it is powerless to follow up the ray of light that has fallen on it, and cast itself into the source. For it is written: 'No one can come to me unless I take him and draw him into myself'.

Mystical bliss is consummated in the consciousness of this gratuitous act, in other words of this supreme dependence upon God.

(Tielhard de Chardin, *Writings in Time of War*, English trans., 1967; pp. 148–9)

But must it be so? Is there not a place for the active quest of the Divine Presence, for taking Heaven by storm? If there is, it will not be found among those mystics who live the institutionalized religious life, but elsewhere.

4 · NON-RELIGIOUS MYSTICISM

This title is not, of course, strictly accurate. There are many records of the experience of exalted states of being by those of little faith or none; indeed, some of them explicitly rejected a religious interpretation of any such experience, as did Shelley in his *Hymn to Intellectual Beauty* – although when he wrote the hymn he had left behind his earlier, avowed atheism and it is debatable whether or not there is, or even could be, a true appreciation of mystical experience in one who denies even the possibility of a supernatural reality in any form. Even so, Shelley's hymn finds an echo in the work of later Nature Mystics; its first stanza is simply descriptive:

> The awful shadow of some unseen Power
>   Floats though unseen among us, – visiting
>   This various world with as inconstant wing
> As summer winds that creep from flower to flower, –
> Like moonbeams that behind some piny mountain shower,
>   It visits with inconstant glance
>   Each human heart and countenance;
> Like hues and harmonies of evening, –
>   Like clouds in starlight widely spread, –
>   Like memory of music fled, –
>   Like aught that for its grace may be
> Dear, and yet dearer for its mystery.

This fleeting sense of something above and beyond us that comes unbidden as an essential part of our reaction to beauty is not, however, of supernatural origin:

> No voice from some sublimer world hath ever
>> To sage or poet these responses given –
>> Therefore the names of Demon, Ghost, and Heaven,
> Remain the records of their vain endeavour,
> Frail spells – whose uttered charm might not avail to sever,
>> From all we hear and all we see,
>> Doubt, chance and mutability.
>
> (From stanza III)

Such a rejection of a divine origin for human exaltation is alien to the work of the mystics we have so far considered – all of whom were publicly committed believers and activists for their faith – but there are, as we shall see, others who are both sharers in Shelley's attitude and yet deserving of the title of mystic.

The experiences of religious mystics are usually sought, either actively or passively; but for many lay people, whether believers or not, exaltation of an analogous kind may come unbidden. This may be in the form of an elation of the spirit which no words can express in adequate form, and which may be an instantaneous reaction to a beautiful landscape, a work of art, a piece of music, or a passage in a book; equally it may follow the sudden, overwhelming awareness of being in love. But although at first there may be no words to describe such a state, we can and do reflect upon it so that eventually we do succeed in recording the content of the experience. The description may not capture its exact nature, nor record precisely our inner state, but, if we are articulate, it will usually be a reasonable approximation: if only because it is a universal human experience that we record. It is something that happens to us, that may even affect the course of our lives, but it is initiated from within our conscious selves as a response to a stimulus in the material world; it may be a door that leads on to other regions of the self, but neither aesthetic sensitivity nor falling in love are mystical experiences. There is no necessary sense of divine presence; of something not of this world.

It is, however, commonly present. C.G. Jung[1] recorded, in his autobiography *Memories, Dreams, Reflections*, visions and other inner experiences that happened to him when he received injections after a heart-attack, and that he could describe 'only as the ecstasy of a non-temporal state in which present, past, and future are one.' As to the source of these experiences, Jung felt that they stemmed from the human soul and whatever unknown, transcendent reality lay behind it: 'It is the psyche which, by the divine creative power inherent in it, makes the metaphysical assertion . . . not only is it the condition of all metaphysical reality, it *is* that reality' (*Psychology and Religion*, collected edition, 1953, para. 836). His view of God was different from that of the overtly religious mystics – 'The experience which I call God is the experience of my own will with respect to another very much stronger will that crosses my path with apparently disastrous results' – and he believed that nothing whatever could be said about the 'metaphysical God'; mystical experiences come from the Unconscious, which is 'simply the medium from which religious experience seems to flow. As to what the further cause of such experience may be, the answer to that lies beyond the range of human knowledge.' (*Civilization in Transition*, collected edition, 1964, para. 565). He did not attempt to draw any conclusions as to the relationship between his experiences and the specific stimulus that led to them – it was, after all, involuntary and occurred while he was unconscious.

Consciously initiating the stimulus that leads to such experiences is, however, a different matter. A response to beauty, whether in nature or in art, may be universal, but the ability to create that beauty is a much rarer gift. All artistic creativity involves mundane elements: for example, the rules of grammar and syntax are essential for the writer, as are a knowledge of materials and the techniques for their use for the artist; but there is also the element of inspiration – the specific choice of words and the order in which they are set down in a poem; the painter's use of line, form and colour in a particular way. These are the individual artist's responses to his or her vision – responses which are less easy to explain in purely material terms.

Such visions are not wholly ineffable, for if they were then the artist would be unable to give them final expression and there would be no art to which we could respond. But the artist may well be aware of his limitations in conveying the vision, as with Arthur Machen (1863–1947), the essayist and novelist, who said of his masterpiece, *The Hill of Dreams*, 'I have seen in the marble, but I have written in the mud.' This same helplessness before the overwhelming experience afflicts all who write of exalted states, but the greater is the writer's literary genius, the closer he comes to the original.

For some writers, whose exalted or ecstatic states have been inspired by the beauty of the natural world, the experience has been of a oneness with Nature that brings with it no sense of a divine presence and may exclude God altogether from the natural order. Richard Jefferies, English naturalist and mystic, felt that 'there is no god in nature' but his experiences were far more than an everyday human response to natural beauty:

> I was utterly alone with the sun and the earth. Lying down on the grass, I spoke in my soul to the earth, the sun, the air, and the distant sea far beyond sight. I thought of the earth's firmness – I felt it bear me up; through the grassy couch came an influence as if I could feel the great earth speaking to me. I thought of the wandering air – its pureness, which is its beauty; the air touched me and gave me something of itself. I spoke to the sea: though so far, in my mind I saw it, green at the rim of the earth and blue in deeper ocean; I desired to have its strength, its mystery and glory. Then I addressed the sun, desiring the soul equivalent of his light and brilliance, his endurance and unwearied race. I turned to the blue heaven over, gazing into its depth, inhaling its exquisite colour and sweetness. The rich blue of the unattainable flower of the sky drew my soul towards it, and there it rested, for pure colour is rest of heart. By all these I prayed; I felt an emotion of the soul beyond all definition; prayer is a puny thing to it, and the word is a rude sign to the feeling, but I know no other.
>
> (*The Story of My Heart*, ed. S.J. Looker, 1947, pp. 20–21)

Jefferies did not believe in an immanent God, and his

mysticism was non-theistic; but his experiences profoundly moved him and he sought for their source:

> I conclude that there is an existence, a something higher than soul – higher, better, and more perfect than deity. Earnestly I pray to find this something better than a god. There is something superior, higher, more good. For this I search, labour, think, and pray. If after all there be nothing, and my soul has to go out like a flame, yet even then I have thought this while it lives. With the whole force of my existence, with the whole force of my thought, mind and soul, I pray to find this Highest Soul, this greater than deity, this better than god. Give me to live the deepest soul-life now and always with this Soul. For want of words I write soul, but I think that it is something beyond soul.
>
> (*The Story of My Heart*, p. 57)

He had glimpsed the Absolute and for all that he denied that it was God, his was unquestionably a true mystical experience, affecting his life and work and disturbing the essence of his being. Jefferies' beliefs were pantheistic rather than atheistic but had clear traditional roots – as can be seen in his relating his feelings to the four elements of Earth, Air, Fire and Water – while other Nature Mystics, such as Walt Whitman and Edward Carpenter, were avowed Pantheists. But not all writers inspired by nature rejected a personal God.

Arthur Machen was a devout Anglo-Catholic for all of his life, but the feelings of awe and the ecstatic states that the grandeur of his native Wales inspired in him were equally as powerful and as effective in moulding his work as those that came upon Jefferies. It is not, however, in his lyrical descriptions of landscape or in the consummate skill with which he evokes the spirit of place that his own mystical experiences are to be found; they are related to his esoteric adventures. Once he was adjured to 'remember that nothing exists which is not God' – a notion that he rejected until:

> Looking back, I believe that, as a child, I realised something of the spirit of the mystic injunction. Everywhere, through the darkness and the mists of the childish understanding, and yet by the light of the child's illumination, I saw *latens deitas*; the whole earth, down to the very pebbles was but the veil of a quickening and adorable mystery.
>
> (*Far Off Things*, 1922, p. 26)

Elsewhere he describes the state in which he found himself when trying to ease his anguish after his wife's death by a form of self-hypnosis. He had become frightened by the process and broke it off, but:

> I found to my utter amazement that everything within had been changed. Amazement; for the utmost that I had hoped from my experiment was a temporary dulling of the consciousness, a brief opium oblivion of my troubles. And what I received was not mere dull lack of painful sensation, but a peace of the spirit that was quite ineffable, a knowledge that all hurts and doles and wounds were healed, that that which was broken was reunited. Everything, of body and of mind, was resolved into an infinite and an exquisite delight; into a joy so great that – let this be duly noted – it became almost intolerable in its ecstasy. I remember thinking at the time: 'There is wine so strong that no earthly vessels can hold it': joy threatened to become an agony, that must shatter all. . . . For that day and for many days afterwards I was dissolved in bliss, into a sort of rapture of life which has no parallel that I can think of, which has, therefore, no analogies by which it may be made more plain.
>
> (Arthur Machen, *Things Near and Far*, 1923, p. 137)

And here again is the great problem that the mystics face: how do we communicate the ineffable? We know, for we assume that Machen is telling the truth, that he had such an experience, but we do not know what it was like. Perhaps prose is not the best medium for conveying the nature of the mystical state in words, for poets seem to have greater success in expressing their experiences than do other writers. But much of that success can become failure if the poet's words are translated into another tongue, and for this reason I have largely confined my examples of mystical verse to poets who have written in the English language. It does not follow that the ecstasy or exaltation expressed by a poet is necessarily a mystical experience, and because similar forms of words may be used in both mystical and non-mystical poems it is necessary to select the former by looking for an extra devotional content and by taking account of the expressed or known beliefs and lives of the poets concerned.

Themes of the transcendence and immanence of God; of selflessness, or surrender to God; and of the Divine Vision are found in a multitude of poems, but the *experience* of Reality, of God is less often found. Henry Vaughan[2] describes it in *The World*, where he says,

> I saw Eternity the other night
>> Like a great *Ring* of pure and endless light,
> All calm, as it was bright,
> And round beneath it, Time in hours, days, years
>> Driv'n by the spheres
> Like a vast shadow mov'd, In which the world
>> And all her train were hurl'd;

But most of mankind does not choose to rise up to Eternity, and Vaughan berates them:

> O fools (said I,) thus to prefer dark night
>> Before true light,
> To live in grots, and caves, and hate the day
>> Because it shews the way,
> The way which from this dead and dark abode
>> Leads up to God,
> A way where you might tread the Sun, and be
>> More bright than he.
> But as I did their madness so discusse
>> One whisper'd thus,
> *This Ring the Bride-groome did for none provide*
>> *But for his bride.*

He has thought that all who will can climb to heaven, but learns that Divine Grace is essential.

The Vision may be lost but can leave a memory in its place; a poor substitute, perhaps, but at least it is proof that the experience *can* be remembered, as in Wordsworth's ode, *Intimations of Immortality*:

> There was a time when meadow, grove and stream,
>> The earth, and every common sight,
>>> To me did seem
>> Apparelled in celestial light,
> The glory and the freshness of a dream.
> It is not now as it hath been of yore; —

Turn wheresoe'er I may,
 By night or day,
The things which I have seen I now can see no more.
 The Rainbow comes and goes,
 And lovely is the Rose,

 The Moon doth with delight
Look round her when the heavens are bare,
  Waters on a starry night
  Are beautiful and fair;
 The sunshine is a glorious birth;
 But yet I know, where'er I go,
That there hath past away a glory from the earth.

For other, more certainly believing poets, their exaltation springs from an awareness of the immanence of God, and the best of them can convey this through their words and the images that they conjure up. Thus it is with Gerard Manley Hopkins in *God's Grandeur*:

The world is charged with the grandeur of God.
 It will flame out, like shining from shook foil;
 It gathers to a greatness, like the ooze of oil
Crushed. Why do men then now not reck his rod?
 Generations have trod, have trod, have trod;
 And all is seared with trade; bleared, smeared with toil;
 And wears man's smudge and shares man's smell: the soil
Is bare now, nor can foot feel, being shod.

And for all this, nature is never spent;
 There lives the dearest freshness deep down things;
And though the last lights off the black West went
 Oh, morning, at the brown brink eastward, springs –
Because the Holy Ghost over the bent
 World broods with warm breast and with ah! bright wings

Not all mystical poets are concerned with the natural world, but for most there is a need to relate the transcendent experience with the world we live in. And this, perhaps, separates poems truly called mystical from those which concern themselves with philosophical speculation or experiences that are indeed religious but that are without either the Vision or the Union, as with that most ubiquitous of 'mystical' poems, Francis Thompson's *The Hound of Heaven*.

More clearly holding the essence of the mystical state is R.S. Thomas's *In a Country Church* (Published by Collins. Reproduced by kind permission of R.S. Thomas.), with its echoes of the ecstasy of St John Vianney's poor peasant:

> To one kneeling down no word came,
> Only the wind's song, saddening the lips
> Of the grave saints, rigid in glass;
> Or the dry whisper of unseen wings,
> Bats not angels, in the high roof.
>
> Was he balked by silence? He kneeled long,
> And saw love in a dark crown
> Of thorns blazing, and a winter tree
> Golden with fruit of a man's body.

But both of these poems are by priests and cannot strictly be said to be part of the non-religious mystical tradition, for all that it is the poetry and not theological language that conveys the experience. One more poem, by the Indian, Rabindranath Tagore (1861–1941) will suffice to show how a sense of oneness with Nature – and thus with the Absolute – is expressed in poetic form:

Autumn

Today the peace of autumn pervades the world.
In the radiant noon, silent and motionless, the wide stillness rests
  like a tired bird spreading over the deserted fields to all horizons
  its wings of golden green.
Today the thin thread of the river flows without song,
  leaving no mark on its sandy banks.
The many distant villages bask in the sun with eyes
  closed in idle and languid slumber.
In the stillness I hear in every blade of grass, in every
  speck of dust, in every part of my own body, in the visible
  and invisible worlds, in the planets, the sun, and the stars, the
  joyous dance of the atoms through endless time – the myriad
  murmuring waves of Rhythm surrounding Thy throne.

All of the 'literary mystics' (which, for want of a better term, they may as well be called) aim at affecting the feelings, emotions and will of the reader, and thus to convey intact their own sense of exaltation or ecstasy. Poetry may be the most successful means of doing this, but they may also use prose to great effect, as with Thomas Traherne in the seventeenth century. Speaking of the innate wonder-vision of the child, which he saw as a 'Gift of God', Traherne says that:

> They are unattainable by book, and therefore I will teach them by experience. Pray for them earnestly: for they will make you angelical, and wholly celestial. Certainly Adam in Paradise had not more sweet and curious apprehensions of the world, than when I was a child.

He recalled his experience much as did Arthur Machen two centuries later:

> All appeared new, and strange at first, inexpressibly rare and delightful and beautiful. I was a little stranger, which at my entrance into the world was saluted and surrounded with innumerable joys. My knowledge was Divine. I knew by intuition those things which since my Apostasy, I collected again by the highest reason. My very ignorance was advantageous. I seemed as one brought into the Estate of Innocence. All things were spotless and pure and glorious: yea, and infinitely mine, and joyful and precious. I knew not that there were any sins, or complaints or laws. I dreamed not of poverties, contentions or vices. All tears and quarrels were hidden from mine eyes. Everything was at rest, free and immortal. I knew nothing of sickness or death or rents or exaction, either for tribute or bread. In the absence of these I was entertained like an Angel with the works of God in their splendour and glory, I saw all in the peace of Eden; Heaven and Earth did sing my Creator's praises, and could not make more melody to Adam than to me. All Time was Eternity, and a perpetual Sabbath. Is it not strange, that an infant should be heir of the whole World, and see those mysteries which the books of the learned never unfold?
>
> (Thomas Traherne, *Centuries of Meditations*, ed. P. Dobell, 1908, 3:2, pp. 151–2)

As Traherne says, one cannot attain the mystical state by reading about it; but there are many who have actively sought such experience, earnestly and devoutly, and who have yet failed to attain it. Why this should be so we do not know – although we should be no more surprised than to find that not all runners can achieve a four-minute mile; we may have ambition but we do not all have sufficient ability – but it is one reason for the mystic's sense of duty: he must provide a vicarious experience for those who are unable to follow him. The point is implicit in an analogy from the writings of Sir Francis Younghusband[3] of the light of the sun and the glory of the Spirit:

> With our bodily eye we cannot bear to look straight at the sun and are provided with eyelids to protect us from its radiance. But we can see enough to be assured of the beauty which light reveals. And those who are just beginning to develop eyes of the soul tell us how blinding is the glory of the Spirit. They cannot endure to gaze upon it. But of its existence, of the joy it can give, and of its priceless value, they are more certain than of anything else in life. Those with souls sensitive enough can feel an influence from above, and be certain of its glory.
>
> (F. Younghusband, *Life in the Stars*, 1927, pp. 200–201)

Elsewhere Younghusband, whose own awareness of the Absolute was stimulated by the vast emptiness and loneliness of the Central Asian deserts, related the recorded experiences of the mystics to his own esoteric and highly unorthodox theological speculations. Nor was he alone in such activity; there is another group of mystics, not religious, nor 'literary' nor Nature Mystics, who have recorded their own experiences and related them to those of others who have followed a similar path: the way of the Secret Tradition. These were not in the strict sense non-religious mystics, but they were (and are) certainly unorthodox, expressing a clear belief in God and suggesting a way of attainment, but a way quite distinct from that of orthodoxy. And while I concentrate on those to be found buried deep within the Christian tradition it must be borne in mind that they are found also hidden within other religious traditions. I have called them 'Esoteric Mystics' which is in many ways unsatisfactory (for one thing it is a tautology) but no other word for them exists.

5 · ESOTERIC MYSTICISM

I have said that mystics of this type follow the way of the Secret Tradition; but what *is* that tradition? It has been defined methodically, and for once in his works, succinctly, by A.E. Waite[1], who wrote that, 'The Secret Tradition is the immemorial knowledge concerning man's way of return whence he came by a method of the inward life.' He added that it:

> contains firstly, the memorials of a loss which has befallen humanity; and, secondly, the records of a restitution in respect of that which was lost . . . the keepers of the tradition perpetuated it in secret by means of Instituted Mysteries and cryptic literature. (*The Secret Tradition in Freemasonry*, 1911, Vol. 1, p. ix; Vol. 2, p. 379)

These, then, are its essential features: a realization that man has lost his awareness of, and entry into a primeval paradise, coupled with a recognition that there is a way of regaining this paradisal state through methods preserved down the ages in 'secret' texts, and practised by those who can correctly interpret those texts. It provides, in effect, a practical way to exaltation of the Spirit and to Divine Union by means other than those offered by orthodox religion – but, as a consequence, it is often rejected and condemned by orthodoxy, as is the case with heterodox Islamic sects and some of the Tantric sects within Buddhism and Hinduism. In the West it found its clearest symbolic expression in the spiritual alchemy that arose from the chaos of post-Reformation science; 'clearest' but by no means clear, although as Waite says of it, 'in respect of its more exalted part it does not differ in term from all spiritual traditions.'

The language of spiritual alchemy was used extensively by Jacob Boehme, but in his hands it becomes wholly Christocentric and there is no alternative application of his words to the work of the practical chemist. He cannot, with any justice, be called an 'esoteric mystic' Two examples will make this clear; the first is from *Concerning the Election of Grace* and the second from *Six Theosophick Points*:

> In that manner as precious pure gold lieth and groweth in a gross, drossy, dirty stone, wherein the drossiness helpeth to work, though it be not at all like the gold; so also must the earthly body help to generate Christ in itself.

> The will is the *mysterium magnum*, the great mystery of all wonders and secrets, and yet it driveth forth itself, through the *imagination* of the desiring hunger, into substance. It is the original of nature; its desire maketh a representation; this *representation* is no other than the will of the desire, yet the desire maketh in the will such a substance as the will in itself is. The true *Magia* is no substance, but the desiring *spirit* of substance; it is an unsubstantial *matrix*, and revealeth or manifesteth itself in substance. The *Magia* is a spirit, and the substance is its body. The *Magia* is the greatest hidden secret, for it is *above* Nature; it maketh Nature according to the form of its will.

Difficult though Boehme is to understand he is yet a truly religious mystic and we find meaning in his words even if it is not at a conscious level. With his odd English followers, this is not so; Dr John Pordage (1607–81) the English divine, for example, rejected the notion of Hell (which Boehme cheerfully maintained) and offered an optimistic view of the workings of Divine Love:

Love is of a transmuting and transforming Nature. The great effect of Love is to turn all things into its own Nature, which is all goodness, sweetness, and perfection. This is that Divine Power which turns Water into Wine, Sorrow and Hellish Anguish into exulting and triumphing Joy; Curse into Blessing; where it meets with a barren heathy Desart it transmutes it into a Paradise of delights; yea, it changeth evil to good and all imperfection into perfection. It restores that which is fallen and degenerated to its primary Beauty, Excellence and Perfection. It is the Divine Stone, the White Stone with a Name written on it, which none knows but him that hath it . . . the Divine Elixir whose transforming power and efficacy nothing can withstand.

(*Theologia Mystica*, 1683, p. 81)

Whatever this is, it is not the product of a profound mystical experience; Pordage was an enthusiast and ecstatic, often in trouble with his neighbours for his excessive religiosity, and his book, according to the Quaker scholar, Rufus Jones, is 'the work of a confused mind, and its spiritual penetration, as also its mastery of the English language, are of a low order.'

The same cannot be said of the one example of true spiritual alchemy that I shall give. I draw it from Thomas Vaughan's *Lumen de Lumine*, or a *New Magical Light*, (1651) for he is one of the few alchemists of this kind who wrote in English, and it is interesting to compare him with both Traherne and Machen, for all three were deeply affected both by the world of nature and by the *genius loci* of the Welsh borderland in which they grew up. Vaughan works first through an allegorical dialogue with Thalia, the spirit of Nature, and then through a bewildering collection of alchemical, kabbalistic and Rosicrucian imagery. Eventually he arrives at the stage of 'The Regeneration, Ascent and Glorification' which he describes in this way:

I have now sufficiently and fully discovered the principles of our chaos. In the next place I will show you how you are to use them. You must unite them to a new life, and they will be regenerated by Water and the Spirit. These two are in all things; they are placed there by God Himself, according to that speech of Trismegistus: 'Each thing whatsoever hath within itself the seed of its regeneration.' Proceed then patiently, but not manually.

> The work is performed by an invisible artist, for there is a secret incubation of the Spirit of God upon Nature. You must not only see that the outward heat fails not, but with the subject itself you have no more to do than the mother hath with the child that is in her womb. The two former principles perform all; the Spirit makes use of the water to purge and wash his body; and He will bring it at the last to a celestial, immortal constitution. Do not you think this impossible. Remember that in the incarnation of Jesus Christ the *Quarternarius*, or four elements as men call them, were united to their Eternal Unity and *Ternarius*. Three and four make seven; this Septenary is the true Sabbath, the Rest of God into which the creature shall enter. This is the best and greatest manuduction that I can give you. In a word, salvation itself is nothing but transmutation.
>
> (Thomas Vaughan, *Lumen de Lumine*, edition of 1910, pp. 77–8)

On the surface this language, which is typical of the whole work, is quite incomprehensible, but possessed of a key to alchemical symbolism, the reader can unlock its meaning and follow the practical process towards Divine Union. Or he could have done with the world-view of the mid-seventeenth century; today it would be next to impossible to maintain the appropriate mind-set even if one had the key. There have been a few, however, – a very few – who have penetrated the dense verbiage of alchemy and reached the ecstatic state that Vaughan himself attained (as we know that he did from his *Memoriae Sacrum*) Two of these were women, one of them (Mrs Atwood[2]) being the teacher of the other (Isabelle de Steiger[3]), but while their undoubted attainment of an exalted state entitles them to the name of 'mystic', it did not bring them the ability to write in words of clear meaning.

In one of her less opaque comments (in her *Memorabilia*) Mrs Atwood envisaged the mystical state as having an element to it that would interact with the physical body, similar in effect, as far as one can tell, to the mesmeric fluid of animal magnetism:

> The handling of the Matter is this, that when the Matter flows forth exteriorly from the new-born consciousness, it passes out into the hand and flows through the fingers, and is able to ferment another life and bring it into the same consciousness; this in turn

rises higher, and is able to re-act, raising again that other which raised it.

But it is nowhere made clear in her works just *how* the exaltation of consciousness is attained. Mme de Steiger is no better – she says of the First Matter that 'It is a cube, perfect, clear, Adamantine, of no known substance; it is not this, not that but yet most common. This enigma-like description is, however, correct, for it embraces all things' – and gives no direct instruction of the kind one would expect from a Spiritual Director. What the alchemists spoke of was the descent of the Divine Light into human consciousness, but they believed the process to be of such great spiritual power that they must not reveal it except in coded form, and many of their codes have still to be broken.

The question that rises from all this was formulated by A.E. Waite, who asked:

> whether there is a mystic secret, the existence of which can and should be intimated, but is at the same time too vital to speak of openly – either from the danger which may attach to it – apart from certain conditions – or from its possible abuse, either because it is only transmitted by initiation or because its expression is not possible in the terms of the logical understanding'.
>
> (Introduction to Thomas Vaughan, *Lumen de Lumine*, p. xlvii).

His unwritten answer was that there *is* such a secret. For the esoteric mystics in general this was the secret of Regeneration: the spiritual purification of Man and his reunion with God, in this world as opposed to the next. The great problem is, as Eckartshausen put it, that 'mere physical man is, in general spiritually blind, having his interior eye closed, and this again is one of the consequences of the Fall.' Thus divine redemption is necessary and also a conscious choosing of the path of Regeneration; only then are we on the way to attainment.

The method is set out by the French mystic Saint-Martin, the 'Unknown Philosopher'. It is simply to seek for God within the self:

> The knowledge which might formerly be transmitted in writing depended on instructions which sometimes rested on certain

mysterious practices and ceremonies, the value of which was more a matter of opinion or habit than of reality, and sometimes rested on occult practices and spiritual operations, the details of which it would have been dangerous to transmit to the vulgar, or to ignorant and ill-intentioned men. The subject which engages us, not resting on such bases, is not exposed to similar dangers. The only initiation which I preach and seek with all the ardour of my soul is that by which we enter into the heart of God and make God's heart enter into us, there to form an indissoluble marriage, which will make us the friend, brother and spouse of our Divine Redeemer. There is no other mystery to arrive at this holy initiation than to go more and more down into the depths of our being and not let go till we can bring forth the living vivifying root, because then all the fruit which we ought to bear, according to our kind, will be produced within us and without us naturally.

('*Selections from the . . . correspondence between Louis Claude de Saint-Martin and Kirchberger, Baron de Liebistorf*; trans. and ed. by E.B. Penny, 1863; Letter CX, pp. 374–375)

Saint-Martin had, in his earlier years, taken part in the rituals designed by Martines de Pasqually and it is these – which aspired to the vision of the human form of Christ – to which he refers. Not all of his fellow mystics would agree that such ceremonies and such initiations should be rejected in favour of contemplative prayer.

In his comments on Thomas Vaughan, Waite was coy about answering his own question concerning the transmission of the 'mystic secret' by means of initiation; in private he was more open: there *is* such a way, leading to the Divine Vision and the Divine Union with the aid of ceremonial workings. And it was a way that he himself followed.

Waite's ceremonies were derived from those of the Hermetic Order of the Golden Dawn, which offered occult doctrines and practices in a systematic, ritualized form for those willing and able to receive them. But Waite transformed the ceremonies so that the participants aspired to self-surrender in God; a very different end from that of the magicians who sought self-understanding and self-fulfilment, with the emphasis very much on the 'self'. The same symbols, of the Rose and the Cross, were used both in the old Golden Dawn and in Waite's Order, but he had restored the wholly Christian content that was in the original Rosicrucian[4] manifestos (the first of which, the *Fama*, is an allegory of the life of Christ), and added a new ingredient: the ascent of the Tree of Life was now an ascent to Christ.

In one of his ceremonies the participants make use of both Rosicrucian and alchemical imagery; the interplay of light and darkness; incense; music – at one point, 'a breathing of slow music, which rises by degrees to a very torrent of sound', to be followed by a chanted hymn – and contemplation in silence and darkness. Theatrical as it may seem, the effect was powerful in the extreme and by the admission of those who were present, it did lead to the experiences of the Vision and the Union.

But although this is undoubtedly a way to the Divine Presence, it is an unknown realm, far removed from traditional mystical practices, whether Christian or otherwise. It does, however, serve to remind us that there is a fine dividing line between true mysticism and false. Waite's intentions and methods were alike positive and healthy, but they were close to more dubious paths which lead away from Reality to illusion and ultimately to self-destruction. Distasteful though it may be we must also look at the dark side of spirituality, at the aberrations of the Mystic Way and the danger into which they can lead us.

6 · FALSE MYSTICISM
THE PATH TO THE ABYSS

At this point it is worth considering the human response to the divine that underlies mystical experience. It is analysed in detail by Rudolf Otto in his study of what constitutes the holy and the manner in which we react to it. Powerful religious emotion contains one element that is 'the deepest and most fundamental'; this, says Otto, is the *mysterium tremendum*:

> The feeling of it may at times come sweeping like a gentle tide, pervading the mind with a tranquil mood of deepest worship. It may pass over into a more set and lasting attitude of the soul, continuing, as it were, thrillingly vibrant and resonant, until at last it dies away and the soul resumes its 'profane', non-religious mood of everyday experience. It may burst in sudden eruption up from the depths of the soul with spasms and convulsions, or lead to the strangest excitements, to intoxicated frenzy, to transport, and to ecstasy. It has its wild and demonic forms and can sink to an almost grisly horror and shuddering. It has its crude, barbaric antecedents and early manifestations, and again it may be developed into something beautiful and pure and glorious. It may become the hushed, trembling, and speechless humility of the creature in the presence of – whom

or what? In the presence of that which is a *Mystery* inexpressible
and above all creatures.
(Rudolf Otto, *The Idea of the Holy*, English trans., 1923, pp. 12–13)

We shall return to the work of Otto in later chapters, but
here we are concerned with the darker workings of the
mysterium tremendum, with the 'spasms and convulsions',
the 'intoxicated frenzy' and its 'wild and demonic forms'
– and also with more subtle perversions of the mystical
experience.

There is a dark side to all mystical experience: the inner
changes in consciousness are necessarily reflected by neurophysiological changes which may or may not find expression
in outward behaviour. Just as such neural alteration may
be subtle – a brief imbalance of body chemistry – so may
behavioural changes be so slight as to be barely perceptible;
or they may affect the mystic but not an observer, as in
rapture or trance; or they may be major and dramatic,
involving convulsions or such violent bodily changes as the
appearance of stigmata (i.e. the replication of the wounds of
Christ, in hands, feet and side, on the body of the mystic.)

That such phenomena may have a purely human origin
has long been recognized, but religious authorities have
been reluctant to accept that the mystics who are seen
as champions of the faith may exhibit the outward signs
of psychological imbalance or of psychosomatic disorder.
One reason for their reluctance has been the tendency for
the medical profession to dismiss all mystics as neurotics
or psychotics because their behaviour mirrors, on occasion,
that of the mentally ill. It may well be the case that there are
behavioural parallels between mysticism and madness, but it
is unwise in the extreme to assume that common symptoms
indicate a common cause, and we should remember that the
belief system of materialist psychiatrists (whether Freudian
or Behaviourist) requires a rejection of anything that cannot
be reduced to an empirical source, for otherwise their carefully contrived world-view falls to pieces.

Equally we should be aware that an admission on the part
of the religious hierarchy that their saints may have been

deluded or hallucinated undermines the structure (if not the foundations) of their faith. But is a balanced view possible? Can the essence of the mystical experience be separated from any physical phenomena that may accompany it?

First let us consider what those physical phenomena are. Montague Summers, in his book on *The Physical Phenomena of Mysticism* (1950), listed them under nineteen headings, but of these, seven (ecstasies, visions, dreams, supernatural knowledge, discernment of spirits, the Fire of Love, and mystical marriage) are purely subjective, while others are varieties of psychic phenomena (such as levitation, bilocation, luminescence, telekinesis and similar powers, clairvoyance, and spiritual healing) or categories that also include clinical symptoms of behavioural or psychosomatic disorder (trance, stigmatization, insomnia, and prolonged abstinence from food.) All that remain are 'Demoniacal Molestations' – which could equally be called poltergeist activity – and incorruption of the body which might be miraculous but is irrelevant to the experiences of a living mystic.

Nor is it easy to see how any of these phenomena can aid the mystic in his quest for Divine Union. They may follow the mystical experience, or even, in the case of ecstasy or trance, precede it, but they are neither necessary nor sufficient conditions for the experience to occur, or once having occurred, to render it valid. Some mystics do report objective physical phenomena connected with their experiences but it is by no means universal. In terms of Christian (specifically Roman Catholic) theology these are:

> *accidental* phenomena of the mystical life, by which we mean those *marvellous phenomena* that, without being confused with contemplation, often accompany it in different degrees, for its outward manifestation'
>
> (Mgr Albert Farges, *Mystical Phenomena*, English trans. 1926, p. 317)

Farges was at great pains to emphasize that 'mystical sanctity' should be 'clearly distinguished from the marvellous phenomena which are often added to it as its complement', and thus, if we allow:

> That such and such a saint might have been hysterical and that such and such an extraordinary detail in his life could be explained as being due to this nervous malady, that would not interfere with his sanctity, which is not incompatible with any malady, and would in no way diminish the other marvellous facts of his life.
>
> *(Mystical Phenomena*, pp. 320–321)

This may well be the case, but the external phenomena do tend to deflect attention away from the essential content of the mystical experience and give a false picture of mysticism to both sceptic and believer. St Teresa of Avila, who experienced trances, raptures, dreams, visions and stigmata (although in her case this was internal) during her religious life, took a common-sense view of these physical phenomena. Although they are in her view divine 'favours', they are designed to 'strengthen our weakness' and she advises her companions that 'we should desire and engage in prayer, not for our enjoyment, but for the sake of acquiring this strength which fits us for service' (*Interior Castle*, VII: iv). She did not, it must be stressed, belittle physical phenomena – her ecstatic vision in which an angel pierced her heart with 'a long golden spear' with a fiery tip, left her 'completely afire with a great love for God', and although 'the pain was so sharp that it made me utter several moans', 'so excessive was the sweetness caused me by this intense pain that one can never wish to lose it, nor will one's soul be content with anything less than God' – but relegated it to a status below that of the inner experience.

A wiser course would have been to eschew physical phenomena altogether. It must be stressed again that whatever their source they are wholly unnecessary as accompaniments of true mystical experience. That they do occur is unquestioned, but it is most probable that they are a result of internal processes within the mystic rather than as a result of divine intervention. In some cases they probably originate in redirected sexual energy, which can also be a source for some of the imagery in the visions reported by the more florid celibate mystics. This particular field is still little known, as was noted by A.E. Waite, who commented that 'Celibacy, for example, accomplished a most peculiar work – of which we as yet understand too little – by the transfer of repressed and starved sexuality to a spiritual plane.' (*The Way of Divine Union*, 1915, pp. 151–152.) Nor does this apply only to Christian spirituality; a similar transfer probably lies behind the use of erotic imagery by the ascetics who practise Tantric Buddhism.

In his book *Mysticism, Sacred and Profane* (1957), R.C. Zaehner argues vehemently that all 'praeternatural phenomena', both external and internal, have no place in mystical experience:

> The experience has nothing to do with visions, auditions, locutions, telepathy, telekinesis, or any other praeternatural phenomenon which may be experienced by saint and sinner alike and which are usually connected with an hysterical temperament. It is true that some advanced (and canonized) mystics have been subject to these disturbances, but they have no essential connexion with the mystical experience itself, the essence and keynote of which is union. Praeternatural phenomena that may or may not accompany it are subsidiary, accidental, parasitic.
>
> (p. 32)

Zaehner's point of view has been endorsed by W.T. Stacc who argued that it was also the opinion generally held by the great mystics themselves, who, he states, 'have often been subject to visions and voices, but have usually discounted them as of doubtful value or importance and at any rate as not to be confused with genuine mystical experience' (*Mysticism and Philosophy*, 1961, p. 47). But this is not a stance that has been universally accepted; for example, Geoffrey Parrinder claimed Jesus as a visionary mystic *par excellence*, and argued that both his experiences and those of St Paul justified one in denoting physical phenomena – in appropriate circumstances – as truly mystical. But this requires a wilful misreading of the Gospels and a confusion between prophetic vision and the experiences of the mystic. And as in Christianity, so in other religions. The sacred dance (the whirling) of the Sufis is partly symbolic and partly a means of attaining ecstasy, it does not follow from the ecstasy. Similarly, the ecstatic dancing found among the Hasidim is an expression of joy at the Divine Presence, not an automatic and unconscious reaction to it. Nor is the wonder-working that often forms a part of the lives of Tibetan lamas seen as in any way essential to their holiness.

It may seem that I am labouring this point, but it is important to stress that true mystical experience does not need the presence of either internal or external psychic or physical phenomena that are properly in the province of psychical research and psychiatry. Equally, their presence should not be taken to imply mental illness or behavioural disorder, however much psychiatric students of mysticism may wish to argue that it does.

Such an argument depends very much on a highly selective choice of words and on their subsequent manipulation. Thus, Scharfstein (in *Mystical Experience*, 1973) claims that while

mysticism is normal everywhere ... it also merges into psychosis. There have been many psychotic mystics and mystical psychotics, assuming that these categories can really be distinguished from one another. It seems to me, then, that mysticism takes abnormal, that is, psychotic forms everywhere.

(p. 133)

Now psychoses are those mental illnesses that involve gross disorder of perception (hallucinations) and thought (delusions), with the result that the psychotic cannot distinguish between fantasy and reality, and suffers a consequent severe impairment of his or her ability to cope adequately with everyday life and normal social relationships. This is not, however, either an accurate or adequate definition of a mystic.

Even so, Scharfstein (and he is only one example among many) ignores both the normality of the mystic's lifestyle and the internal consistency of the philosophical interpretations he may place upon his experiences. Among other inanities, he states that:

Even apart from hallucinations, we ought not to hesitate to

71

classify such influential mystics as Swedenborg or Boehme among the paranoids [i.e. one who exhibits systematized delusions of grandeur and persecution], though they may, like many other psychotics, have said penetrating things and had powerful fantasies . . .

(*Mystical Experience*, p. 133)

Apart from the fact that Swedenborg was not a mystic, this dogmatic statement fails to convince because neither man was hallucinated: one was a visionary who built a theological system from visions that he never claimed were a part of the material world, while the other created a complex and systematic cosmogony subsequent to his mystical experiences. Both men also lived rational, respectable and thoroughly normal lives. Scharfstein goes on to compare the well-documented psychotic hallucinations of such men as Daniel Schreber, (the paranoid judge, whose case and 'memoirs' were discussed by Freud) with the visionary experiences of the mystics. But Schreber's hallucinations and delusions clearly relate to this world and are as clearly seen to be unreal and empirically impossible; they show all the hallmarks of thought disorder, unreason and destructive, disturbed behaviour. Against this the mystic's experiences are unusual rather than abnormal; he does not see the world as unreal (which Scharfstein claims that he does) nor does he believe that his exalted experiences are events in the material world; and he continues to lead a balanced and well-adjusted life in which delusions concerning the world about him do not figure.

Other points argued in the attempt to identify mystical experience with psychosis are the depersonalization (the loss of a sense of identity) and loss of a sense of time that are allegedly common to both. But while these effects cause pain and anxiety to the psychotic, and have neither meaning nor purpose, they form part of a blissful, unitive experience for the mystic. The psychotic retains his fear and anguish when the experience fades, while the mystic is stimulated to selfless activity – his moral imperatives are reinforced and he has clear goals in sight.

It must be admitted that some of the more florid

manifestations of religiosity in the sixteenth and seventeenth centuries undoubtedly involved psychosomatic disorders in disturbed individuals, but the fact that an uncritical church hierarchy at the time saw signs of sanctity in such behaviour does not justify us (as it did not justify them) in labelling them mystics. Mysticism and mental illness have little in common save that both are even now far from fully understood. They do, however, have one factor in common: explanations for both have been sought through the medium of drugs.

The religious use of intoxicants, narcotics and mind-altering drugs has a long and dishonourable history, from the unidentified Soma of the Vedas, through the Bacchic Mysteries and the hashish-taking of the Assassins, to the peyote-induced visions of the Native American Church.[1] Whether or not the effects of such drug-taking are comparable to mystical experience is a question that has, for the last half-century, generated vehement debate.

In 1954 Aldous Huxley experimented, under more or less controlled conditions, with the hallucinogenic drug Mescalin. He interpreted the experience as being truly mystical:

> The Beatific Vision, *Sat Chit Ananda*, Being-Awareness-Bliss – for the first time I understood, not on the verbal level, not by inchoate hints or at a distance, but precisely and completely what those prodigious syllables referred to.
>
> (*The Doors of Perception*, 1954, p. 13)

His sensory impressions, especially vision, were intensified and he experienced a sense of timelessness, but he noted also that while his intellect seemed to be unimpaired, his will suffered 'a profound change for the worse'; nothing seemed to be worth doing, and the mescalin taker 'finds most of the causes for which, at ordinary times, he was prepared to act and suffer, profoundly uninteresting. He can't be bothered with them, for the good reason that he has better things to think about.' (*The Doors of Perception*, p. 19.) This hardly conforms to the attitudes and actions of the mystic, as Huxley eventually came to realize.

73

What Huxley's writings on the drug experience principally convey is confusion of thought, but at the end of his life he came to recognize that he had inflated the value of his own experience, that he was not acting as some cosmic being but that his insight was 'the most dangerous of errors ... inasmuch as one was worshipping oneself.' He went on in more modest fashion:

> We must learn to come to reality without the enchanter's wand and his book of the words. One must find a way of being in this world while not being of it. A way of living in time without being completely swallowed up by time.
>
> (Laura Huxley, *This Timeless Moment*, 1968, pp. 269 & 290)

Other enthusiasts for the use of mind-expanding, or psychedelic, drugs made even wilder claims. Timothy Leary believed that by taking LSD (lysergic acid diethylamide) he reached up to and experienced God – albeit with fanciful language:

> God does exist and is to me this energy process; the language of God is the DNA code. Beyond that, the language of God is the atom. Above that, the language of God is the exquisite, carefully worked out dialogue of the planets and the galaxies, etc. And it does exist and there is an intelligence and there is a planfulness and a wisdom and power that you can tune in to. Men have called this process, for lack of a better word, 'God'.
>
> (*The Politics of Ecstasy*, 1970, p. 223)

According to Leary it is LSD that will bring us union with God and it is best accomplished during sexual union, because LSD is not only consciousness expanding, but is also 'the most powerful aphrodisiac ever discovered by man.' God and sex together are the fruits of Dr Leary's tree, and it must be admitted that he has recognized the parallels between the mystical experience and sexual ecstasy; what he does not notice is that the language of sexual union is employed by the mystics because it is the only universal analogy of mystical union in human experience.

Eventually Leary condemned the use of psychedelic drugs (perhaps only because of the imprisonment it brought him) but more rational voices than his had endorsed the drug experience. During Easter of 1962 Dr Walter Pahnke carried out an experiment on a group of theological students at Harvard, in which ten took a dose of psilocybin (which is similar to LSD) while another ten took a placebo – none of them knowing which they were taking. All of them then listened to the Good Friday sermon and sat quietly afterwards. Nearly all of the psilocybin group (compared with just one from the control group) reported having religious experiences conforming to the categories laid down by W.T. Stace (which are discussed in the next chapter). From this experiment Pahnke deduced that the students *did* have valid mystical experiences; a conclusion endorsed by Stace who later said of the drug experience, 'It's not a matter of its being *similar* to mystical experience; it *is* mystical experience.' (Quoted in Zaehner, *Drugs, Mysticism and Make-believe*, 1972, p. 79.)

But what were those experiences like? One of the students is quoted, from Pahnke's unpublished thesis, by Masters and Houston in their classic work, *The Varieties of Psychedelic Experience* (1966): 'I felt a deep union with God ... I carried my Bible to the altar and tried to preach. The only words I mumbled were peace, peace, peace. I felt I was communicating beyond words.' But not presumably to the benefit of his hearers. Such preaching should be contrasted with the sermons of Meister Eckhart or the letters of St Teresa of Avila; the qualitative difference is immediately apparent and one feels certain that however elevated was the experience of Dr Pahnke's student it lacked more than a little of what the mystics clearly possess.

Zaehner was avowedly antagonistic to the notion that psychedelic drug experiences had more than a superficial resemblance to mystical experiences; he had tried mescalin for himself with results quite different from Huxley's:

It was interesting and it certainly seemed hilariously funny. All along, however, I felt that the experience was in a sense 'anti-religious', I mean, not conformable with religious experience or in the same category. In Huxley's terminology 'self-transcendence' of a sort did take place, but transcendence into a world of farcical meaninglessness.

(*Mysticism, Sacred and Profane*, 1957, p. 226)

Others who began from a position of believing in the substantial identity of psychedelic ecstasy and mystical experience changed their opinions over time.

Carlos Castaneda ended his mescalin experiments with the Yaqui Indian, Don Juan, frightened by the experience; many of the visions were terrifying and held a nightmare quality that convinced him that he would not gain enlightenment by such means. Robert Masters and his wife, Jean Houston, deplored the casual and often inaccurate use of Eastern religious terminology by enthusiasts for psychedelic exploration. They pointed out that:

> Mystics and religious personalities have repeatedly warned against accepting states of sensory and psychological alteration or visionary phenomena as identical with the depths of the spiritual consciousness. These warnings go unheeded today by many investigators of the psychedelic experience who seem to accept the subject's experiences of heightened empathy and increased sensory awareness as proofs of religious enlightenment. Doubtless some of these experiences are analogous in some way to religious and mystical experiences. But religious analogues are still not religious experiences. At best they are but stages on the way.
>
> ('op. cit' p. 258)

And one further point should be borne in mind: many drugs are addictive, and dependence upon a drug belies the illusion of inner freedom that it may give, and *all* drugs, whether narcotics, hallucinogenics or stimulants such as alcohol, are toxic. Poisoning the body is not the best of ways to a fuller life or liberation of the spirit.

Some, however, would not agree. In the popular mind drug-taking is associated with the murkier areas of occultism, in particular with the perversions of magic that have stemmed from the work of Aleister Crowley (1875–1947), one man who did believe that drug-taking could lead to expansion of consciousness and to ultimate enlightenment. Few objective students of either magic or mysticism would agree with him, but the questions remain of the relationship between the two and the nature of magical attainment.

Definitions of magic tend to be as vague as those of mysticism, from Crowley's inadequate 'Magick is the Science and Art of causing Change to occur in conformity with Will', to Eliphas Lévi's all-encompassing 'traditional science of the Secrets of Nature', or the dictionary suggestion that it is 'the art that purports to control or forecast natural events, effects, or forces by invoking the supernatural.' Evelyn Underhill offered a more complex but generally more satisfying definition:

> Magic, in its uncorrupted form, claims to be a practical, intellectual, highly individualistic science; working towards the declared end of enlarging the sphere on which the human will can work, and obtaining experimental knowledge of planes of being usually regarded as transcendental . . .
>
> (*Mysticism*, 1930, 12th ed., p. 152)

She also had the advantage of having made the transition from a practical and theoretical experience of magic (during her time in the Golden Dawn) to a similar experience of mysticism.

The important words in Miss Underhill's definition are, 'in its uncorrupted form' and we should recognize that not all present-day practitioners of magic conform to the popular image of the black magician – a conflation of Crowley in fact and Dennis Wheatley in fiction. What must be recognized is the distinction between the Hermetic and the Rosicrucian approach to magic. It was well expressed by Gerald Yorke, who wrote:

> Now Hermetic Orders as such are only Christian in that they include some Christianity but do not stress it. Rosicrucian Orders on the other hand are primarily Christian but draw on pre-Christian sources. In other words the Hermetists always try to become God in his anthropomorphic or in some instances theriomorphic form. They inflame themselves with prayer until they become Adonai the Lord . . . whereas the Christian approached God the Father through Christ (Adonai) but never tried to become Christ, only to become as Christ.
>
> (Quoted in K. Raine, *Yeats, the Tarot and the Golden Dawn*, 1972, p. 13)

Building on this, one may say that the Rosicrucian approach is the way of mysticism, while the Hermetist follows a magical way that is anything but mystical.

Evelyn Underhill puts the distinction more succinctly: 'The fundamental difference between the two is this: magic wants to get, mysticism wants to give – immortal and antagonistic attitudes, which turn up under one disguise or another in every age of thought.' She continues:

> In mysticism the will is united with the emotions in an im-passioned desire to transcend the sense-world, in order that the self may be joined by love to the one eternal and ultimate Object of love; ... this is the poetic and religious tempera-ment acting upon the plane of reality. In magic, the will unites with the intellect in an impassioned desire for super-sensible knowledge. This is the intellectual, aggressive, and scientific temperament trying to extend its field of conscious-ness, until it includes the supersensual world: obviously the antithesis of mysticism, though often adopting its title and style.
>
> (*Mysticism*, 1930, 12th edn, p. 71)

Essentially, then, magic[2] differs from mysticism in its aims and object – it is centred on the self for the benefit of the self, seeking exalted experiences for self-satisfaction only, with no intention of serving others or of submitting to the divine will. And because it is difficult to admit to oneself that the final goal is self-satisfaction, magicians tend to aggrandize their work. Israel Regardie says of Magic that it is 'a quest spiritual and divine ... a task of self-creation and reintegration, the bringing into human life of something eternal and enduring'. (*The Tree of Life*, 1932, p. 31.) This would be appropriate if he was writing of mysticism but he proceeds to offer practices that inflate the ego and glorify the self; magic is also the path of self-delusion.

For A.E. Waite, magical practices were separated abso-lutely from mysticism: 'phenomenal occultism and all its arts [i.e. magic] indifferently connect with the tradition of the mystics: they are the path of illusion by which the psychic nature of man enters that other path which goes down into the abyss.' (*Ceremonial Magic*, 1911, p.ix.) In this he echoes the far older warning contained in the *Chaldean Oracles*:

> Stoop not down into the Darkly-Splendid World; wherein continually lieth a faithless Depth, and Hades wrapped in clouds, delighting in unintelligible images, precipitous, winding, a black ever-rolling Abyss; ever espousing a Body unluminous, formless and void.
>
> (Ed. by W.Wynn Westcott, 1895, p. 46)

Such images are an emphatic reversal of the light that is the essence of the Divine Vision of the mystic.

And if magic is the antithesis of true mysticism, it is not alone. Much of 'occultism' so called, and many of the pseudo-cults imported into the West by gurus of doubtful spirituality and equally doubtful morals, also have no claim to the label 'mysticism'. They offer self-indulgence and self-aggrandisement which do not form a part of the mystic way; their cry is not 'eternity now' but 'satisfaction now'. Not that the mystic is world denying, but neither is he content with the world of sense perception; his final goal is Divine Union, but on the way he gives rather than takes. As with much else, so in mysticism: By their fruits shall you know them, and when the fruits of magic are not illusory, they are self-destructive.

7 · THE NATURE OF THE MYSTICAL EXPERIENCE

We have seen that definitions of mysticism are notoriously difficult to make in any meaningful way; they may be implicitly sceptical, as in that quoted by Parrinder, which is also restrictive: 'belief in the possibility of union with the Divine nature by means of ecstatic contemplation' (*Mysticism in the World's Religions*, 1976 p. 12), or explicitly theistic, as with Dean Inge's 'Mysticism means communion with God, that is to say with a Being conceived of as the supreme and ultimate reality.' But neither of these takes us very far forward: they are concerned solely with religious mysticism, they take no account of other forms of mystical experience or of other paths to the goal of union, and they do not approach the problem of setting out the distinguishing features of the mystical experience that set it apart from other 'altered states of consciousness'.

That term itself is question-begging, and it would, perhaps, be better to substitute 'transcendental' for 'altered'. This was suggested by Julian Silverman, who wrote:

The term 'altered states of consciousness' has been applied to states other than the ordinary waking state. 'Altered' is, for me, a misleading term. It would be better if, instead of this word, some more neutral symbol were used to denote other states of consciousness, because the word 'altered' leads to the unfortunate notion that all other states are deviations from the ordinary waking state. To regard organismic events in this way is, in effect, to judge them rather than merely to describe them. A kind of psychological chauvinism has been the result.

('On the Sensory Bases of Transcendental States of Consciousness', in S.R Dean (ed.), *Psychiatry and Mysticism*, 1975, p. 368)

He suggested 'transcendental' because it has been defined as 'being beyond the rational, remote from practical affairs or from human comprehension', and 'Any of the non-ordinary states of consciousness referred to as "altered" fits at least part of this definition.'

The original term was defined by Charles Tart in this way:

An altered state of consciousness for a given individual is one in which he clearly feels a *qualitative* shift in his pattern of mental functioning, that is, he feels not just a quantitative shift (more or less alert, more or less visual imagery, sharper or duller, etc.), but also that some quality or qualities of his mental processes are *different*. Mental functions operate that do not operate at all ordinarily, perceptual qualities appear that have no normal counterparts, and so forth.

C. Tart (ed.), *Altered States of Consciousness*, 1972, pp. 1–2)

There are many such states, but they can be classified according to the way in which they are produced: they may involve reduced sensory stimulation and motor activity, or a considerable increase of these; they may follow increased alertness or mental involvement, or a decrease in these; or they may be due to alterations in body chemistry and neurophysiological changes – which may be involuntary or reduced. Mystical states are generally preceded by decreased alertness, reduction of physical activity and external stimuli, and a passive state of mind – but such states, or at least their analogues, can also follow intense activity or induced neurochemical changes. Transcendental states of consciousness (as I prefer to call them) in general tend to share certain characteristics, some (but not all) of which are usually present in mystical states. These have been categorized by Arnold Ludwig (in C. Tart (ed.), *Altered States of Consciousness*, pp. 15–20) and include, alterations in thinking; disturbed time sense; change in emotional expression; body image change; perceptual distortions; change in meaning or significance; a sense of the ineffable; and a sense of rejuvenation. Two other factors – loss of control and hypersuggestibility – do not usually apply in mystical states unless the mystic is 'surrendering to God', but this is a conscious and voluntary giving up of the self, not a loss of self-control.

The looseness of definition of mysticism, coupled with a prevailing materialist philosophy, has led some observers and investigators to consider the mystical state as *abnormal* rather than unusual or non-ordinary, and even to deny that transcendental states can occur spontaneously in the normal population. Thus a survey in 1960 of American college students which found that 39 per cent of the group surveyed had spontaneously experienced, in the waking state, a significant alteration in their sense of reality (i.e. a state of depersonalization), was dismissed on the grounds that 'brief, repetitive, depersonalization cannot occur in the general population as frequently as it did in this sample. If it did so, its existence would have been recognized and its incidence acknowledged in the literature.' (Silverman, in C. Tart (ed.), *Altered States of Consciousness*, 1972, p. 367.) Two further surveys found that 46 per cent of their samples – of 'normal, non-psychedelic-drug-using, young people' – reported similar experiences. The incidence of such states has also been confirmed by the work of Sir Alister Hardy's Religious Experience Research Unit, (Now called the Alister Hardy Research Centre) at Westminster College, Oxford.

But we have still not arrived at a final definition of mysticism and the mystical experience. To be adequate this must take account of the consequences of the experience in terms of its effect upon the mystic, and to incorporate this into our definition is next to impossible. Rufus Jones, the great Quaker student of mysticism – who was also a mystic himself – commented on this:

No definition of religious mysticism in general abstract terms is ever satisfactory. At its best it misses the vivid reality of a genuine mystical experience, somewhat as one misses the reality of motion when one stops a spinning top to see what motion is like! In both cases, what we are endeavouring to examine eludes us. In one instance we are examining an arrested object in order to find out what motion is like, and in the other instance we are putting an abstract theory in the place of a palpitating human experience which flowers or may flower into an endless variety of forms and types. It involves the fallacy of substitution – putting dry, congealed words for the live pluckings of the heart.

(*The Flowering of Mysticism*, 1939, p. 250)

His comments apply with equal force to other forms of mysticism – if any of them are, indeed, truly non-religious. Perhaps we should opt for brevity and use the narrow definition of Frederick Streng (in S.T. Katz, *Mysticism and Philosophical Analysis*, 1978, p. 142) Mysticism, he says, is 'an interior illumination of reality that results in ultimate freedom.' This will not satisfy everyone but at least it does take account of the effect of the experience.

Having settled, however uneasily, what mysticism *is*, we must now consider how its different forms are distinguished; what are its principal features; and how it is experienced. There is, as we shall see, no agreement among scholars over these issues and there are no final answers.

The questions of Nature Mysticism and of various pseudo-mystical states have already been discussed, but it as well to distinguish the former from religious mysticism. Both have traits in common, but while the religious mystic seeks direct union with God, the nature mystic, in the words of Rudolf Otto, has 'the sense of being immersed in the oneness of nature, so that man feels all the individuality, all the peculiarity of natural things in himself', and 'the divine One is reached and experienced in the essence and joy of nature' (*Mysticism East and West*, 1932, p. 74). He ought to have added that not all nature mystics accept that there is a 'divine One'; for many of them there is no God other than the totality of the material universe.

Nor is religious mysticism all of a piece. Within theistic

religions the union of man with God requires the action of Divine Grace, but in monistic religions (such as that of Sankaracharya) divine union comes about through an illuminating realization of the true nature of the self. Even ecstasy, which might be thought of as the same experience whatever the context, has been divided; Rufus Jones considered the ecstatic, self-negating absorption into the One to be akin to a pathological state of trance. For him the true ecstasy of the mystic was:

> . . . a type of ecstatic state, of inspiration and illumination, which seems to me to be a most glorious attainment and very near to the goal of life – a state of concentration, of unification, of liberation, of discovery, of heightened and intensified powers, and, withal, a burst of joy, of rapture and of radiance . . .
>
> (*Rufus Jones, The Flowering of Mysticism*, 1939, p. 6)

There are, however, a number of characteristics common to all forms of the mystical experience, which have been summarized by W.T. Stace. He set out the following seven characteristics (here slightly abridged):

1. The Unitary Consciousness, from which all the multiplicity of sensuous or conceptual or other empirical content has been excluded, so that there remains only a void and empty unity. This is the one basic, essential, nuclear characteristic, from which most of the others inevitably follow.
2. Being nonspatial and nontemporal. This of course follows from the nuclear characteristic just listed.
3. Sense of objectivity or reality.
4. Feelings of blessedness, joy, peace, happiness, etc.
5. Feeling that what is apprehended is holy, sacred, or divine.
6. Paradoxicality.
7. Alleged by mystics to be ineffable, incapable of being described in words, etc.

> (*Mysticism and Philosophy*, 1960, p. 79)

Stace calls this the 'universal core' of mystical experience, and his analysis has been widely accepted, but it is necessary also to consider the way in which these experiences are reported. Three different categories of mystical writing have been distinguished:

1   Autobiographical reports of specific instances or types of mystical experience.

2.   Impersonal accounts, not necessarily based exclusively upon the writer's own experiences, in which mystical experience tends to be described in generalized and abstract terms.

3.   Accounts of a mainly theological or liturgical kind which although referring to some mystical object or reality do not refer, unless very obliquely, to mystical experience itself.

(Peter Moore, 'Mystical Experience, Mystical Doctrine, Mystical Technique', in S.T. Katz, *Mysticism and Philosophical Analysis*, 1978, p. 103)

Of these, only the first two are directly concerned with mystical experience, and they contain, in Moore's analysis, four distinct elements: (a) retrospective interpretation (doctrinal interpretations of the experience after it has happened); (b) reflexive interpretation (spontaneous interpretations made during or immediately after the experience); (c) incorporated interpretation (features of the experience caused or conditioned by the mystic's prior beliefs, aims and expectations); (d) raw experience (those features unaffected by the mystic's prior beliefs, etc.)

For the reader who is concerned with mysticism itself, rather than with purely academic verbal gymnastics, it will be enough to be aware of these analyses and to apply them to mystical texts only as and when they so wish. The point to be made is that such texts can be and have been systematically analysed in order that the experiences they report and interpret may be the better understood.

Of more immediate concern to such mystically inclined readers will be the effects of the experience on the mystics themselves. It is, above all, a holistic experience: not only is the whole body-mind-spirit continuum of the mystic affected, but his whole life also. The consequences of the experience – especially when it comes unsought – can be profound: there may be a new or radically changed sense of the purpose and meaning of life (as happened with Jacob Boehme), or there may be changes in attitudes to others and even in previously held religious beliefs. The latter effects are equally true of the conversion experience; this also is a direct awareness of, and surrender to God, and the whole life of the convert is consequently changed. The most dramatic example of this is the conversion of St Paul, which is not demeaned if it is taken to have occurred during an epileptic fit, for the same areas of the brain appear to be involved in both epilepsy and the transmission to neural pathways of mystical or other transcendental experiences. In the conversion experience, as in the mystical, there is the same fervour and desire to share the experience with others; but the mystic does not normally take the same theological stance of stressing the severity rather than the love of God, nor does he demonstrate the same abasement before God that is characteristic of the convert (and this seems to apply equally within Christianity and Islam; converts to non-theistic religions appear largely to have moved in response to intellectual stimuli rather than emotional ones, and, consequently, they rarely display the same sort of fervour.)

We accept, then, that the mystical experience happens, and that it affects the whole man: if it affected only the non-empirical part (the spirit, or soul) then the mystic would have no memory of it, for memory depends on neuronal pathways in the physical brain, and he could give no account whatever of it; he would not even be aware that it had happened. Equally, if it was solely a physical experience within the body-mind continuum, then it would have no 'moral' content – there would be no sense of a duty imposed – and it is clear that this is an important element of the experience. A.E. Waite expressed it thus: 'And those who enter into this state come back into the world, with the yoke of the kingdom upon them in a law of service. Then God shall give them work' (Lamps of Western Mysticism, 1923, p. 329.)

It is not enough for us, however, to know that it happens, we wish to know also how it happens – what sets off the experience – what are the immediate and ultimate sources of the experience, how the mystic is aware of it and how (if at all) he is able to describe all that is happening to him. Providing answers to these questions requires the language and methods of many disciplines – theology, philosophy, psychology and physiology, among others – and even then our answers will often be no more than hesitant and tentative.

We do know many of the stimuli that may lead to transcendental states of consciousness; they have been described in detail by Marghanita Laski (in *Ecstasy: a study of some secular and religious experiences*, 1961) and by Sir Alister Hardy (in *The Spiritual Nature of Man*, 1979), both of whom recorded and analysed in depth large numbers of these experiences. Miss Laski labelled the specific stimuli that she identified as 'triggers' and included aspects of nature (commonly water and heights; trees, flowers and their scent; sunrise and sunset); music; poetry; pictorial art; architecture (especially churches); creative work; and sexual love. A somewhat different, but analogous set of triggers was given by Hardy, who listed natural beauty; sacred places; prayer, meditation and worship; the visual and auditory arts; literature in various forms; and sex and personal relationships. Both authors added other, minor, triggers and a series of negative triggers in cases where the experiences had followed sorrow, despair and stress. In all, they offer almost the whole of human experience as a fruitful source for potential stimuli for attaining transcendental states of consciousness. One does not question either their intentions or the accuracy of their reports, but they did not consider in any depth the question of a predisposition to respond to such stimuli on the part of their subjects.

We ought to ask why certain stimuli trigger ecstatic, religious or mystical experiences in some people but not in others. Miss Laski argues that whereas withdrawal experiences (she divides ecstatic experiences into two kinds) can be deliberately induced, intensity experiences cannot; and yet she also states that 'I think it probable that all intensity experiences begin by being, to no matter how slight a degree, withdrawal ones.' (*Ecstasy*, 1961, p. 369.) This suggests that there is at least *some* prior movement towards the transcendental state on the part of the person experiencing it, which fits with the reports of Christian, Muslim and Jewish mystics who invariably speak (in however convoluted a manner) of actively seeking God before their experiences began. Given that the predisposition exists, the mystic (or would-be mystic) then has the experience triggered by a stimulus whose specific nature depends on his personality, his upbringing, and his religious and social cultural background. It will be a profitable exercise if we reflect on what would be appropriate triggers for ourselves.

And once set off, where within us does the experience take place? In a sense it envelops us both within and without, but our awareness of the event is a function of our consciousness, which is mediated (located, if one is a thorough-going materialist) in the brain, although the mediator may be said more accurately to be the mind. This, for the mystic, is something more than our thinking, feeling and willing processes: 'The nature of mind', said the Zen master, Xu Yun, 'when understood, no human words can encompass or disclose.' Some, however, have tried.

For A.E. Waite, Divine Union, which is 'realization in God', can be obtained only by an act of Mind. He does not mean, however, the mind as the rational, thinking part of our being, but as:

> the state of pure intelligence in deep contemplation [which] is a state of essential love in the highest, as at an apex of Mind. The Mind is love, the Mind is high desire, the Mind is Soul, unless we talk of the Soul as a kind of psychic body or vesture of the next life: in this case Mind is Spirit.

And, he maintains, we can know God only by way of the Mind:

> 'All whatsoever which we know, shall and can know of God, lies within these measures – the measures of human Mind. It follows that the search after God is a Quest in our own being; and, linea media or otherwise, supposing that there is a way to God, this way is within. The reason is that obviously there can be no other, seeing that it is we who ascend the heights, as it is we who explore the deeps.
>
> (Shadows of Life and Thought, 1938, pp. 238, 237)

We may not agree completely with Waite's definition of mind, but he is undoubtedly right in placing the quest within:

we go inwards in search of God, who is working outwards to us from the very centre of our own being. Our real problem is not in having the experience and knowing that we have had it, but in transmitting the experience to others in a meaningful way, for it is not an experience that is amenable to description or even interpretation in everyday language. The mystic may use the vocabulary of sense experience to describe the experience but the words must take on shades of meaning quite distinct from their ordinary use.

The reason for this lies in the often repeated claim that mystical experience is ineffable: that it *cannot* be communicated, from its very nature. This, however, is simply not true – if it were so then every mystic would be struck dumb and we would have no literature of mysticism; there would be only the 'meaningless noise' that Bertrand Russell believed was the sole content of non-empirical discourse. What the mystics are trying to say is that their inner experiences, which they feel a compulsion to express as fully as may be possible, cannot be related in everyday speech, and as there is no distinct, coherent, and internally consistent language for experiences with no true sensory counterpart, they must use such linguistic devices as simile, metaphor and paradox, however inadequate these may be for the task.

Limited ineffability there certainly is; Arthur Koestler referred in just such terms to an experience of non-existence that happened while he was imprisoned during the Spanish Civil War: 'When I say "the I had ceased to exist" I refer to a concrete experience that is verbally as incommunicable as the feeling aroused by a piano concerto, yet just as real – only much more real.' We can approach his experience through his analogy and through his stress on its intensity, but we cannot get to the core because that is pre-eminently *his* experience that can never be ours; we may have similar experiences, but if we know them to be of the same order it is not by means of words.

The mystics frequently attempt to convey the content of their experiences by means of paradox (for example, 'I both exist and do not exist', 'I am united with God and yet distinct from him') and this has as frequently

89

been used as a justification for denying the validity of the experience: paradoxes are illogical; mystical experience is expressed in paradoxes; therefore mystical experience is illogical (followed by the unstated conclusion that, being illogical, mysticism does not exist and the mystic is deluded). This syllogism is itself quite valid and the logician is entitled to deny the truth of mystical paradoxes; but he tends also to deny them any meaning and in this he is in error: in terms of their usual meaning the statements within the paradox may be false, and the laws of logic may be quite properly used to determine the truth or falsity of those statements – but meaning is not the province of logic and we may justly conclude only that the paradoxical statements of mysticism are non-logical, not that they are without meaning.

Having thus set up and knocked down the straw-man logician, we are still faced with the problem of the mystic's use of words. If logic does not apply to the language of mystical experience, then what does? The mystics speak to us and, in some manner, we understand what they say; but this must be a non-rational mode of thought on our part as far as the experience itself goes – for the mystic can only speak of it *after* it has ceased to happen, a point that was made by Plotinus, who said: 'In this apprehension we have neither power nor time to say anything about it. Afterwards we can reason about it.' And we who listen can understand the reasoning, even if it is non-logical. It is most effective and, perhaps, most comprehensible when it is put into poetical form, for it is a gift of the poet that he can convey sublimity in a manner with which we empathize even if the words do violence to reason. Such is Lao Tze's account of Tao:

> When you look at it you cannot see it;
> It is called formless.
> When you listen to it you cannot hear it;
> It is called soundless.
> When you try to seize it you cannot hold it;
> It is called subtle.
> No one can measure these three to their ultimate ends,
> Therefore they are fused to one.
>
> It is up, but it is not brightened;

It is down, but it is not obscured.
It stretches endlessly,
And no name is to be given.
It returns to nothingness.
It is called formless form, shapeless shape.
It is called the intangible.
You face it but you cannot see its front.
You follow it but you cannot see its back.
Holding on to the Ancient Way (*Tao*)
You control beings of today.
Thus you know the beginning of things,
Which is the essence of the Way (*Tao-Chi*)

> (Trans. by D.T. Suzuki in his *Mysticism: Christian and Buddhist*, 1979, p. 12)

Suzuki argued forcefully that words are inappropriate to convey the mystical experience:

Our language is the product of a world of numbers and individuals, of yesterdays and todays and tomorrows, and is most usefully applicable to this world. But our experiences have it that our world extends beyond that, there is another called by Buddhists a 'transcendental world' and that when language is forced to be used for things of this [transcendental] world, it becomes warped and assumes all kinds of crookedness: oxymora, paradoxes, contradictions, contortions, absurdities, oddities, ambiguities, and irrationalities. Language itself is not to be blamed for it. It is we ourselves who, ignorant of its proper functions, try to apply it to that for which it was never intended. More than this, we make fools of ourselves by denying the reality of a transcendental world.

> (*Mysticism: Christian and Buddhist*, 1979, p. 40)

Perhaps, then, we should not try to respond intellectually to the mystical experience, however much we may justly apply reason to interpretations and analyses of the experiences, and to the philosophies of mysticism constructed upon them. In the absence of words we may simply react with elation – as do the Hasidim when they dance for joy at the presence of God, and the Sufis when music stirs their hearts to seek God. We shall consider this again when we examine the various means by which the mystic seeks to convey *his* experiences to us; now we must seek an answer to the question of the ultimate source, a question put comprehensively by R.E.L. Masters and Jean Houston, who framed it in such a way as to include all (or nearly all) possible answers:

> Still the question remains: Where is this information coming from? Is it a gift of God? of Grace? of hyper-neuronal ecstasy? Is it a result of our twelve billion brain cells astronomically interconnecting at the speed of light and now galvanized by a psychedelic drug to ever more prodigious computations – to tune in finally on the Process Itself? Or perhaps may it be, as some theorists propose, that the cell has its knowledge that Knowledge does not know? In regard to this last suggested explanation, it might be argued that it is a well-known fact of biophysics that there is a kind of purposiveness to all bodily processes, be they ever so microscopic. It might be, then, that in the sensitized psychedelic state the subject picks up some sense of this purposiveness from his physical processes which he then dramatizes in terms of the drama of birth, growth, decay, and death. Or could it even be that the subject becomes aware of the purposiveness and then transforms this insight into a scientific spectacular from information dimly remembered or subliminally recorded?
>
> (*The Varieties of Psychedelic Experience*, 1966, p. 305)

From which piece of wholly sensory language we may move to the source of our senses – to the brain, where if one cannot find the mystical experience, one can at least follow the neuronal dance it sets in motion. But just *how* this elusive state of consciousness interacts with the brain cells is a philosophical problem which may finally prove to be insoluble, as the psychiatrist Jan Ehrenwald believes:

> We must realise that there is an irreducible gap in our ultimate understanding of how neurophysiological processes are converted into conscious perceptions, or how they trigger acts of volition. The gap, in what can be described as the autopsychic sphere, is admittedly small and usually ignored or glossed over by both scientists and laymen. It is more conspicuous and much larger on the psi level or in the heteropsychic sphere. But it is essentially of the same order.
>
> ('The Non-Euclidian Mind' in R.S. Dean ed., *Psychiatry and Mysticism*, 1975, p. 67)

Perhaps we should not ask 'where does the mystical experience come from?' but rather 'what changes does it bring about in the brain?' Those at least we can measure, and we know that they must be made in order for the mystic to be able to express in visual, aural or other sensory form, the insights, thoughts and feelings that the experience engenders in him.

In the history of mysticism it is well attested that of the great mystics who have recorded their experiences, only women – with the one significant exception of St Ignatius Loyola – have been visionaries. This is not to say that they have been hysterics or otherwise unbalanced – they have not – but among them St Hildegarde of Bingen, the twelfth-century German mystic, clearly incorporated abstract visual configurations that are commonly associated with migraine. From this one can deduce that the neurophysiological counterpart of their visual experiences is located in the occipital lobe of the cerebral cortex, which mediates visual impressions.

It is also known that in very general terms the left hemisphere of the brain is concerned with language, logical thinking, and calculation, while the right hemisphere is concerned with intuitive thinking, creativity, aesthetic appreciation and spatial perception; which division of function would lead one to expect a greater role for the right hemisphere in mystical experiences. But it is further thought that there is a sexual preference in the brain: the left hemisphere being dominant in men and the right in women. On this basis, if the right hemisphere is significant in mystical experience, there ought to be a sexual imbalance in favour of women in the numbers of mystics – but there is no evidence for this and one must be wary of extravagant claims for the dominant role of the right hemisphere in any transcendental states of consciousness.

Nonetheless, there is neurophysiological evidence – from both electroencephalographic (EEG) studies of Yogis and of Zen priests and disciples, and neurophysiological studies of clinical analogues of the mystic state – that points to specific structures in the brain as mediators of the mystical experience. Both EEG studies observed the appearance and persistence of alpha rhythms in recordings of the subjects' brain activity, even though their eyes were open and they were subject to visual stimuli. This is contrary to what one would expect, as the alpha rhythm, which is associated with a meditative, quiescent state in which the eyes are closed, does not normally occur when there is both attention and arousal in the subject. What was happening in these studies was that the subjects were consciously inhibiting the 'alpha block' (the disappearance of the rhythm when the eyes are opened) when in the state of Satori or of Samadhi; in effect they had disciplined themselves to ignore the visual (and other) stimuli that would in the ordinary state have affected their brain activity. Because visual stimuli are mediated by the occipital cortex we can be quite sure that this area of the brain plays a significant role in the practice of meditation. It is thus reasonable to suppose that it also plays a part in mediating the mystical experience itself.

Evidence from clinical studies is even more specific. If we accept that the auras occurring in epilepsy are more or less accurate analogues of some elements of the mystical experience, then we can also accept that those parts of the brain involved in epilepsy – notably the temporal lobes of the cerebral cortex – are also involved in the neurophysiological mediation of mystical experiences. This has been studied by Dr Peter Fenwick, who has commented:

In the cases reported in the literature, it would appear that, at the time the mystic experiences arise, the discharges [i.e. the epileptic fits] are confined to the non-dominant limbic system [which relays sensory input to the cortex], particularly the medial temporal structures. However, it is clearly too simple just to place the source of mysticism in the right temporal lobe. A reasonable hypothesis would be that the non-dominant temporal lobe is intimately involved with the genesis of mystic experience and adds positive tone to the perception of reality which occurs during the experience itself.

(Quoted in N. Coxhead, *The Relevance of Bliss*, 1985, p. 91)

Other investigators have supported this suggestion of the importance of the temporal lobes in the mediation of mystical states. They have also located other centres in the brain that appear to be involved, notably in the reticular system (a network of cells spread throughout the brain stem), within which are two groups of cells that can modulate inputs to the brain. The rostral reticular system (at the upper end of the brain stem) has connections to all parts of the cerebral cortex, and when its activity increases the whole of the cortex is stimulated. It is itself stimulated particularly by carbon dioxide, so that when carbon dioxide levels are lowered − as in deep or rapid breathing which forms a part of many meditative techniques − cortical activity, and with it responsiveness to sensation, is reduced. The other modulating group of cells is at the bottom of the brain stem and this acts by selectively inhibiting inputs from the peripheral nervous system. Focusing the attention on a single sensory or mental input and reducing reticular activity will thus put the brain into a 'quiet' state and provide an inner environment conducive to mystical experience, and psychological studies have demonstrated clearly that in non-ordinary states of consciousness our attention is 'withdrawn from the environment and is focussed inside on internal happenings'. (Silverman, in C. Tart (ed.), *Altered States of Consciousness*, 1972, p. 374.)

This does not exhaust the theorizing about the location of brain centres involved in such experiences, but other theories are neither generally accepted nor supported as yet by adequate evidence. But neurophysiological and psychological findings now allow us to be certain that specific areas within the brain *are* related to transcendental states of consciousness. What we do not know is whether they are involved in initiating them or are merely responding to some unidentified stimulus working at the level of an interface between the empirical and non-empirical elements of the whole human being.

Perhaps the sequence of events is like this. A non-empirical stimulus leads us actively to seek out a trigger (which may be a prayer, an icon or other pictorial imagery, a sound, a paradoxical ko-an, or any of the whole range of triggers suggested by Laski and by Hardy) which in turn leads us into a state where sensory stimuli are blocked and neural excitation is lowered. At this point neural activity will be in harmony with the working of the will and the Mind (in Waite's sense) and the mystical state may be entered.

One nagging doubt remains. If the mystical experience is transcendental, why do we need the physical element at all? Is it not enough that we have had the experience in our inner, eternal, non-empirical being? It is not, because while we live, we are in the body and it is through the body that we communicate with other human beings. If the mystical experience has a purpose other than self-gratification – and all mystics of every tradition say that it does – then we must be able to express that experience; first to enter it coherently into our own memory store and then to communicate it to others. We have seen the way in which it may be mediated in the brain and we may thus accept that it *can* be stored as a memory, but we are faced with the far greater problem of determining just how the nature and meaning of the specific mystical experience can be passed on to another.

8 · I AND THOU
COMMUNICATING THE MYSTICAL EXPERIENCE

The mystic knows that he has experienced Divine Union – or whatever else he may choose to call it – for there is a memory of the event, or at least a memory that something happened to him, something significant that he must not keep to himself but must give to others as it was given to him. If his memory is accompanied by ecstatic feelings, it may be that the ecstasy is simply a response to the event; not an essential part of it, but rather a part of the neurophysiological events that enable him to form and retain the memory. Nor must it be an undifferentiated memory; he must structure it so that it has a meaning that can be conveyed to another. Both internal structuring and the subsequent communication are difficult tasks.

Little has been written or said as far as the former problem is concerned, but the difficulties surrounding it are implicit in most comments on the seemingly equally insoluble problem of communication. R.E.L. Masters and Jean Houston lamented the difficulty, and although they were referring specifically to the psychedelic drug experience, their remarks are applicable to all transcendental states of consciousness:

Unfortunately, the high emotional content, sense of awe and

reverence, and other elements of a psychedelic subject's religious experience cannot really be conveyed in such a way as to validate the content of the experience so far as a reader is concerned.

(*The Varieties of Psychedelic Experience*, 1966, p. 299)

When he tried to convey his own mystical experiences, A.E. Waite emphasized these difficulties. His account, wordy and convoluted though it is, deserves examination not only because it encapsulates the problems of all mystical description, but also because he did not write from a sectarian viewpoint and thus avoided emotive and potentially divisive words:

There is a state beyond the images, a repose of inward being, apart from action in the mind. . . . In so far as it can pass into expression it is a state of awareness at one's own centre, but it will be seen that the attempted formulation produces an inevitable image in which the essence escapes. There is no realisation therein of centre, circumference, height or deep, and that awareness which is perhaps the only representative word has no relation to things or objects, to modes and qualities, but is wholly and unconditionally within. I suppose that in the nature of things it emerges subsequently in the mind as an awareness in self, but there is no reaction on self or objective presence of the ego. It is not mind reflecting on its own being. Realisation itself is only an approximate word and exceedingly remote also, because it denotes effort, while the state is still being, outside both subject and object, as if in some middle way between this pair of opposites. It is, moreover, neither light nor darkness, which belong to the world of appearances, and it cannot be called knowing, which connotes a faculty in exercise and that upon which it acts. The state knows not this or that.

When it is entered there is no sense of beginning, middle or end, for the state is timeless. It is only on coming out therefrom that the external correspondence in event is found to be exceedingly short. But it must be understood here that in attempting to convey an impression I am under the penalty of words which fail everywhere and communicate nothing but antithesis. The state is not entered and one does not come out therefrom: we are simply in it and subsequently we are not in it, but amidst a terrible experience of lost beatitude in reality.

The sense of abiding in the timeless is not with us and that of beatitude belongs to the subsequent reaction. There is no external correspondence in temporal duration because time does not measure eternity, nor is metaphysical infinity represented by extension in space.

There seems no doubt in experience that the habit of going inward into the state, when we sink willingly therein, may cause it to endure longer in respect of the time-appearance; but the inward reality is one and is not affected thereby. In itself it is full completeness, though time has measured but seconds. If we reflect in the mind thereon, whether in the aftermath or otherwise, it will be seen, I think, that we cannot have more or less of an eternal mode of being.

(A.E. Waite, *Lamps of Western Mysticism*, 1923, pp. 325–6)

The state that Waite describes is clearly far removed from any everyday experience with which we may be familiar, and yet something of its nature *is* conveyed to us. That we can grasp, however fleetingly, the nature of the mystical experience from prosaic descriptions in words designed for other purposes, was recognised by R.C. Zaehner. He was referring to Huxley's mescalin experiments, but his comments have a wider application:

Part of the difficulty is, I suppose, that language has no words with which to describe these prodigies. It has in fact no words with which to describe mystical experiences of any kind. Despite this fact the nature of the particular experience is at least *indicated* by the words used.

(*Mysticism Sacred and Profane*, 1961, p. 7)

Even so, the alleged ineffability of mystical experience becomes real enough for most mystics when they struggle to pin it down. Many of them give up and revert to poetry and paradox, but others persist, and it is they – such as Rumi or Julian of Norwich – who are consequently most accessible to us. Plotinus undoubtedly touched the Absolute, and Eckhart certainly glimpsed it, but their experiences remain somehow distant; there is too much of cold intellectuality about their words – *they* may have been fired by Divine Love but it is their interpretation of that fire that comes across to us, not the fire itself.

And it is precisely because some mystics are able to communicate to us, though whether it is on a level other than that of intellectual understanding must remain an open question, that Stace gave 'alleged ineffability' as one of the characteristics of the experience. He remained sceptical because for all that mystics use such expressions as 'inexpressible', 'unutterable' and 'beyond words', in practice they do describe their experiences in words. R.M. Bucke described his own experience of the state in the preface to his book Cosmic Consciousness:

> All at once, without warning of any kind, he found himself wrapped around as it were by a flame-coloured cloud. For an instant he thought of fire, some sudden conflagration in the great city; the next, he knew that the light was within himself. Directly afterwards came upon him a sense of exultation, of immense joyousness accompanied or immediately followed by an intellectual illumination quite impossible to describe . . .
>
> (Edition of 1969, pp. 9–10)

But not impossible for one to make an attempt at description, for Bucke set out to give fifty examples of 'Cosmic Consciousness' – all codified, annotated and interpreted in some 400 pages of text.

Inability to describe on the part of the mystic is not the same as ineffability, but there must be a reason for the habitual insistence of the mystics on this quality. They believe that their exalted consciousness differs from ordinary consciousness not only in a relative way but in an absolute way: it is not a matter of degree but of essential nature. And they justify their distinction by pointing out that it is they, and not us who have experienced both forms of consciousness, and thus only they who can know the nature of both. They may succeed only partially, or perhaps not at all, in their attempts to convey the nature of their experiences, but this is of less importance to them than it is to us: what they are striving more urgently to do is to convey the meaning of the experience, so that we may believe not only in its reality, but also in its moral and spiritual purposiveness, and thus be led to understand how and why it has effected a profound change in the life of the mystic. Now it may be objected that Nature Mystics, for example, do not attempt to elevate the moral tone of their audience, but their choice of language is invariably designed to encourage a respect and love for the natural world, because of our oneness with it, and this is quite clearly a positive, moral intention.

It may also be the case that the often baffling ambiguity and paradoxicality of mystical texts is of deliberate intent – much in the way that a blocking of rational thought processes may be sought in Zen Buddhism by deliberate confusion of the mind with paradox (as in asking the question, 'What is the sound of one hand clapping?'), in order to achieve a heightened awareness. But if the mystic seeks to communicate with words, there are many problems to overcome, whatever his motive may be.

Mystics are not all of one religion or one culture, and when they do put their experiences into ordinary language it will inevitably be in their own tongue; thus Sankaracharya was recorded in Sanskrit, while Plotinus wrote in Greek, Eckhart in German, and Julian of Norwich in Middle English. We who speak, write and read modern English must have translations of all of these if we are even to begin to make sense of what they are saying to us, and there is thus a triple barrier between us and the original experience. First it must be established in the neural processes of the mystic himself, in order for him to retain his own awareness of the experience; then it must be put into ordinary speech so that it can be recorded and transmitted to the mystic's contemporaries; and finally it must be translated into other languages for the benefit of the rest of humanity. At each stage there is the possibility, to put it no more strongly, that some essential element of the experience will be lost; but in many cases the living spirit of the original texts still survives: a lasting tribute to the dedication of the mystical writers and to the skill of their translators.

There is also the largely ignored question of the dedication and mind-set of the reader. We are eager to learn what the mystics say and we patiently struggle with obscure and difficult texts in order to gain our own enlightenment; something about those texts succeeds in striking a chord within us and we feel an empathy with the writer. But why this should be so – what first sets us off on the quest for attainment of the mystic state – will vary from person to person, although there will always be an acceptance of a reality beyond the phenomenal world, of an ultimate unitive state towards which we can and must strive. If there is no such acceptance and no such dedication, then our reading will be no more than an exercise in literary criticism or an excursion into the byways of philosophy, and we will only marvel at the notion of an ecstasy which must remain, for us, forever without meaning.

But we have accepted the reality and we are dedicated to striving for it, so we may consider just how we can understand it, or rather, what the mystic can do in order for us to understand. If he is using ordinary language he must use the devices of simile, metaphor and paradox – as he did in order for the experience to make sense to himself – and encourage us to use our intuitive faculty to interpret the superlatives by which he expresses profound qualitative differences in the states of being that he describes. This is somewhat simpler for mystics within the eastern traditions, for whom a technical vocabulary, not related to the language of sense-experience, already exists. In the West terms such as *Samadhi, Nirvana, Satori*, or *dhikr*, have no exact equivalents, and such words as we do use tend to have multiple meanings (or shades of meaning) and thus to appear ambiguous. To overcome this the western mystic may resort to poetic techniques: choosing specific imaging words to utilize their rhythms, cadences and sounds in order to stimulate an appropriate response in the reader. This, however, only tends to render translation into other western languages as difficult as, for example, translating Zen koans into English.

Another approach that may be adopted is to associate specific nouns with contradictory adjectives – most commonly associating darkness and light – and thus to produce a paradox. An example of this is the description given by

J.H.M. Whiteman of one of his own mystical experiences; he describes it elsewhere as 'The Vision of Archetypal Light' which powerfully emphasizes its difference but in utilizing paradox he produces a subtle shift in our way of looking at of his experience so that we gain a better understanding of it; during the experience 'there was', he says, 'before my eyes no object distinguishable in light'. He continues:

> But the absence of visual objects does not imply that there was a sense of blindness or of an obstruction in front of the eyes, or that the thought of seeing never entered the mind; for it is possible in such a state to see a certain wonderful darkness or blackness associated with what is too high for one's powers of discernment. So, now, through the eyes came a vision as of the holy stillness of night-time.
>
> ('Thoughts on the Art of Mystical Description', in *Studia Mystica*, I:4, 1978, pp. 66–7)

But paradox may engage the intellect while the mystic is encouraging us to use our intuition, and for this he will do better to emulate the traditions of the East and seek to create new words to represent the phenomena of mysticism. Such words do not suffer from problems of translation as there are no pre-existing equivalents in any other language and they may stand as they are. An example of this is Rudolf Otto's coining of the word *numinous*. Admittedly, Otto was not himself a mystic but he was attempting to pin down a specific element of mystical experience. He was seeking a word that would stand for the non-rational, feeling-response element in the word 'Holy' as opposed to the implicit factor of 'the morally good':

> It is worth while to find a word to stand for this element in isolation, this 'extra' in the meaning of 'holy' above and beyond the meaning of goodness. By means of a special term we shall the better be able, first, to keep the meaning clearly apart and distinct, and second, to apprehend and classify connectedly whatever subordinate forms or stages of development it may show. For this purpose I adopt a word coined from the Latin *numen*.
>
> (Rudolf Otto, *The Idea of the Holy*, 1923, pp. 6–7)

Now this is admirable and Otto's new word has passed into general use in all European languages. But it is difficult to create new words for mystical experience and to apply them retrospectively to the works of mystics of the past; not only does it imply a final understanding of that work when it may still be obscure, but it also fixes that work within the framework of a given modern language, inhibits future translation, and renders null and void all previous commentary upon the text. Contemporary mystics could and should seek for these new words, but in practice they have failed to do so and have turned to other means of communicating the nature and implications of their experiences.

Words are not only written, they are also spoken, and it is likely that mystical experience can more easily be conveyed through speech than through writing, for speech permits all the subtle variations of emphasis, intensity, intonation, stress and volume, as well as changes in facial expression and the added dimension of gesture. Tauler's sermons – which contained far more of the experiential side of mysticism than did those of his immediate predecessor, Eckhart – have the power to move the reader today, but they would certainly have had a far more powerful effect upon his contemporary congregations who could both see and hear him. But the mystic is still bound by the limitations of language: would his voice and gesture convey anything out of the ordinary to us if we could not understand the language in which he spoke? Under the right condition it would, for sounds themselves, devoid of specific associations, can have a significant effect upon the state of mind – even the state of consciousness – of the hearer.

Boehme, George Fox and other seventeenth-century mystics compared the confusion of human language with the 'one tongue and understanding' of the birds, which they looked upon as being like the 'tongue of men and of angels': a language of pure connotation as used by Adam in Eden and by the Disciples at Pentecost; a language that could convey divine truths. They were not alone in this, for the repetition of seemingly meaningless names was used in some Gnostic hymns and invocations as an aid to exaltation of the spirit. But this was not pure sound; in each case both speakers and hearers were presumed to know the language, whereas there are also what Otto calls 'original numinous sounds' which were 'at first inarticulate sounds rather than words.'

The idea that the very sound of the words used in speech can induce ecstasy was utilized by Arthur Machen in *The Hill of Dreams*, the novel into which he incorporated his own early transcendental experiences:

> Language, he understood, was chiefly important for the beauty of its sounds, by its possession of words resonant, glorious to the ear, by its capacity, when exquisitely arranged, of suggesting wonderful and indefinable impressions, perhaps more ravishing and farther removed from the domain of strict thought than the impressions excited by music itself.
>
> (1927 edition, p. 156)

And not merely words that are immediately understood. In one of his essays, 'The Gift of Tongues', Machen tells the story of 'the so-called "Speaking with Tongues" at Bryn Sion Chapel, Treowen, Monmouthshire, on a Christmas Day of the early [18]70s'. The minister, Thomas Beynon, suddenly began to use speech and gestures utterly unknown to his congregation:

> It rang out and soared on high, and fell, to rise again with wonderful modulations; pleading to them and calling them, and summoning them; with the voice of the old *hwyl*, and yet with a new voice that they had never heard before: and all in those sonorous words that they could not understand. They stood up in their wonder, their hearts shaken by the chant; and then the voice died away. It was as still as death in the chapel.
>
> (*The Cosy Room*, 1936, p. 161–2)

What it was, although neither the preacher nor his congregation knew at the time, was the Latin Mass – abhorrent to all of them in its associations but with a power in its form and essence to lift them to another state of being.

Structured in a coherent sequence, sounds become music, and although, for the listener, music alone is unlikely to precipitate the mystical experience itself, it can be extremely effective in bringing about the state of being in which we are open to an understanding of that experience. If, for example, we read a mystical text with the intention of gaining a true insight into its meaning, then music will often be a powerful aid to bringing this about, even though appreciation of music is so intensely personal that we cannot avoid visual, emotional or other associations that tend to distract us from the text in hand. For the performer, however, music may well lead to something akin to the mystical experience itself. Speaking, in a lecture on mysticism and art, of the 'wonderful experience' that may come to a group of musicians playing together, Gustav Holst said:

> If you are all masters of your instruments and of your music – all sure of yourselves and each other – then you may go through an experience about which you will either keep silent or use the language of the Mystics.

This does not, however, help the mystic to convey his message to those of us who have not had his experience. We are unlikely to listen to the living voice of a mystic and as we encounter records of the mystical experience almost exclusively through the written word, most of what has gone before will apply only in an ideal world – in so far as it concerns someone else conveying the essence of an experience to us rather than stimulating an analogous experience in us. Sensory stimulation may well act as a trigger for ourselves, but it will of itself not enlighten us as to what past mystics mean by their words. It may help to arouse emotions that will lead to enlightenment, but inner activity and external stimuli cannot work alone: we must use our intellect also in order to have a certain knowledge, rather than a vague notion of what the mystics mean.

And if we attain that certain knowledge we ourselves have a duty to strive to transmit it to others. This will be no easy task but we might consider what could be done to assist in it. One of the great stumbling-blocks in the way of a universal understanding of mysticism is, as we have seen, the extreme difficulty of translating the technical vocabulary of mysticism in one tradition or culture into that of another.

But although it may be difficult it is not impossible. What is needed is the systematic collection, codification and analysis of every recorded mystical text, with the aim of establishing a common language of mysticism.

Such a gigantic task would require resources that are unlikely to be offered by established religious and educational authorities who have other priorities; if it is ever to be undertaken it must be the work of dedicated individuals who are prepared to labour for no reward, and to renounce individual fame and praise for the benefit of the many. It will require first that the texts in question be analysed in the languages in which they were originally written, and second that they be divided into the three categories of autobiographical report; impersonal account; and theological and philosophical interpretation. Texts belonging to the first two of these would then be collated and common features identified: these being separated into universal common features and features specific to particular faiths, while those features unique to each mystic would be related to his own life-history and cultural background. From all of this detailed analysis there should emerge a picture of the essential nature of the experience of Divine Union – or whatever other expression may best convey the essence of the experience. It would also permit of truly accurate translation of mystical texts from one human language to another.

This, however, concerns the mystic and his personal experience. To further our understanding of the methods of communicating the experience, we would need to examine the influence of each mystic, and to look for records of how his disciples, followers and readers down the centuries came to accept the validity and importance of his work and to propagate his particular message. Once this task has been completed, it should be possible to collate the results, to analyse them, and from the analysis to construct a model of the ideal means of communicating the essential nature of the mystical experience. Beyond this lies the task of making a comparative analysis of the doctrines of the mystics both within their specific faiths and in relation to other faiths. Ultimately this would lead us to finding the common ground of mystical experience in all faiths, and so to the possibility of a universal understanding of what God, the One, the Absolute, Ultimate Reality, or whatever term we may use, truly *is*.

But this can never be a purely intellectual understanding. It must also be experiential, and we must now consider how we can attain that experience – not vicariously through the reports of others, but directly, in our own beings.

9 · THE WAY TO ATTAIN

In one sense mystics are born and not made, but while trouble comes to all men as surely 'as the sparks fly upward', it is equally sure that mystical experience does not come to all; indeed, there is no certainty that it will come to any of us. We may strive for it: we may pray fervently, meditate furiously, or endlessly chant the sacred, rhythmic words that are mantras, but these things will not of themselves bring us face to face with God in a direct, personal experience.

For many of us an enthusiasm for esoteric theories and practices may lead to a genuine interest in meditation and to the systematic practice of particular techniques. We may also desire something more than the relief from stress and sense of personal well-being that such practices bring, but we invariably place the whole activity into just one of the many compartments into which our complex lives are divided, and place a label on it, reading 'Spiritual Life, to be opened on Thursday evenings and Sunday mornings only' – perhaps more, perhaps less, but protests to the contrary ring hollow, for we are all human and all with the same frailties and vanities.

Of course, we must make these efforts, for the practical

techniques are essential, but something more is needed. Above and beyond interest and enthusiasm we must have a true dedication: not one that is centred on the little self and bounded by restless time-watching, but a dedication that reaches into every part of our lives, that recognizes that the Way is a re-ordering of our whole life. It does not demand of us a renunciation of the material world, or the rejection of our everyday lives – equally, it does not deny us that path if we wish it – but it does demand that our commitment to the Way is total, not a daytime dedication that closes down at six o'clock and takes three holidays a year.

We must also be aware that awareness of being committed to a spiritual goal does not bring with it an immediate knowledge of the means to attain that goal. The means we employ will depend partly upon our own nature and personality, and partly upon the cultural milieu in which we have been raised and which will have determined our religious attitudes: we may change (or think we change) our belief system, but the manner in which we express our belief – to ourselves as much as to others – will be a product of our upbringing and environment.

And this is the reason why so much of Eastern spirituality sits so uneasily in Western souls; it is not so much that it is necessarily wrong – questions of religious truth and error are ultimately matters of personal conviction, and, however much we may wish to see the whole world professing Christianity, Buddhism or some other faith, we cannot impose specific doctrines on those who choose to reject them – but that it is alien to our established way of being. Wishing that it was not so will not alter the fact that it *is* so; at some unguessable date in the future, all mankind may think, act and feel in the same manner, but at this time, as in all past time, they do not. One aspect of the divide between East and West was well expressed by Suzuki. Here again is the comment I quoted earlier:

Whenever I see a crucified figure of Christ, I cannot help thinking of the gap that lies deep between Christianity and Buddhism. This gap is symbolic of the psychological division separating the East from the West.

The individual ego asserts itself strongly in the West. In the East, there is no ego. The ego is non-existent, and, therefore, there is no ego to be crucified.

(D.T. Suzuki, *Mysticism Christian and Buddhist*, 1957 p. 94)

We may not agree with Suzuki's opinion, we may feel that time has closed the gap, but he spoke for both his heart and mind; the differences between us need nct divide us one from another as far as tolerance and mutual respect go, but the gap remains and the only rational response to the fact is to accept it, and to work with who we are and the culture and tradition from which we spring.

This is not to say that we cannot modify and use techniques that have come from other traditions, but we must recognize what they are and discard the doctrinal baggage that comes with them. We will find also that many of these techniques have well-established parallels in the West: for example, the use of the mantra. These sacred formulae – there is no limit to their number, for each mantra is supposed to be passed from teacher to pupil for use in his private meditation – are designed as an aid to focusing the attention and to escape from the sensory distractions around one, but they are seen in a more rarefied light in the East; Sri Aurobindo eulogizes rather than defines the mantra when he says that it is, 'a supreme rhythmic language which seizes hold upon all that is finite and brings into each the light and voice of its own infinite.'

The most famous mantra in use today is the syllable AUM, which stands for the Atman, or self, and meditation upon it supposedly leads to liberation from the world, to divine union (with Brahman), and to immortality. But whatever it may do in the East it does not appear to have achieved any of these goals for its eager devotees in the West: and it never will, for it represents a mind set that is not and never can be theirs. It can, however, help them to achieve the lesser but necessary goal of entering a meditative state. Perhaps more useful would be the Jesus Prayer of the Hesychasts – the monks of the Orthodox Church 'who in silence devote themselves to inner recollection and private prayer' – which will, even in the meditator who considers himself no longer Christian but who can yet restrain the desire to condemn his former faith, evoke an inner response from something very close to the core of his being.

Because of this response it is also called the 'Prayer of the Heart' – it is the mood evoked rather than the meaning of the word (or words: its longer form is 'Jesus Christ, Son of God, have mercy on me a sinner') that becomes important. Unlike the chanting of AUM, which aims at ecstasy, the Jesus Prayer is used to attain *hesuchia*, or 'quiet'. The method is that of 'watchfulness' (*nepsis*) which has two stages, that of 'flight' (*phuge*) and that of 'silence' (*sige*): by keeping watch over oneself, one retreats within into an inner silence with the object of attaining the Divine Vision (but not Union). That the method is effective cannot be denied but it utilizes body postures and breathing exercises ('limit the air that passes through your nose so that you are breathing with difficulty') that do not easily lead to relaxation and it will not appeal to all. It does, however, serve to remind us of the importance of silence.

It may be possible for Zen meditators and Indian yogis to shut off awareness of external stimuli (as is shown by their ability to propagate alpha rhythms in the brain even though their eyes are open) but this state is not easily achieved and anything that can be done to reduce sensory input is a help to meditation, and thus to attaining the contemplative states that lie beyond it. Physical relaxation is the first requisite, which in turn demands a comfortable body posture and the reduction of all discordant or inappropriate sensory stimuli. A gradual rather than a sudden disappearance of external stimuli should be the aim; music – if one is listening to it – may come to its natural end, and lights may be lowered, although if it is natural light that is vanishing with the setting sun, one must not forget that heat vanishes with it, and sudden cold produces alarm signals in the skin which have anything but a relaxing effect. Remember to keep the surroundings at an even temperature.

Repetition of a mantra or a prayer need not be aloud and

quiet is more conducive to a meditative state. But it is essential to keep one's senses open and to be aware of, but not responsive to, the stimuli around one: the small sounds; the sensations of one's body and the smell of the room. One is not seeking to lose awareness (and to drop off into a comfortable but scarcely elevating sleep) but to control and direct it.

These introductory suggestions are simple and ought to be commonplace. They set up the conditions in which the mystical experience itself may be sought, but it must be emphasized that a relaxed state of mind, however pleasant, is no more than that: it is not the stillness and silence of contemplation. Meditation involves the stilling of thought by concentrating on, say, a visual or auditory image; in a sense it requires one to look at that image. Contemplation is, if the paradox can be excused, more an active passivity; a recollection of the scattered elements of thought and their focusing upon God.

Intermediate between these two states is that of 'Contemplative Meditation' (or so it is said; I must confess to an inability to identify any precise point where one shades off into another, all that can be said is that one knows when one is in a particular state – pinpointing the shift from one to another is almost impossible; it is also unnecessary). In this state one meditates on the essential content of sentences from sacred texts (generally, but not necessarily, Christian texts) as opposed to the associations that they bring to mind. That is, if I am working with a saying of Christ, I will be still and be aware of what that saying means, rather than trying to put it in context, relating it to my life or that of others, or considering what its practical applications might be. The aim is to become aware of Christ, not as a romantic pictorial image, but as an all-pervading Presence. It is also as well to remember that the aim of such contemplation is not easily attained – disappointment is initially the most likely result. Nonetheless it can be a profitable experience, and for those who feel drawn to it these simple rules may be followed.

DIRECTIONS FOR CONTEMPLATIVE MEDITATION

1.   Sit in a comfortable position, and consciously relax the body but remain upright, with the legs uncrossed and with both feet on the ground. (This prevents muscle strain, cramp and backache).

2.   Repeat the words of the chosen sentence, gently and slowly, and often enough to keep the mind from wandering.

3.   Work with the same sentence for several days, using it frequently throughout the day. If circumstances prevent such use, ensure that the meditation is carried out at the same time each day.

4.   Do not attempt lengthy meditation. It is enough, at first, to meditate for no more than five minutes. With practice the meditation can be successfully continued, but never for more than twenty minutes.

5.   When coming out of the meditative state, stay quiet and relaxed for a further five minutes in order to reflect on the experience and to adjust to the everyday world.

For those who wish to chart their progress through this and other forms of meditation and contemplation, the following direction is also appropriate:

6.   Record the experience: your recollection of it and your thoughts and feelings about it. If it is practised in a group, record it first and then discuss it.

This exercise is offered as one example of a specific method of carrying out Contemplative Meditation; while it can lead to a mystical experience, there is no guarantee that it will do so. Those who wish to try it may find it beneficial, but it is not in any sense a divine ordinance; there is no single path to attaining the mystical experience and it must always be borne in mind that every path is no more than a means to an end. It is all too easy to become so involved in the practical techniques that the goal is forgotten: awareness of being *in* a transcendental state of consciousness (whether or not it is truly mystical) is *always* more important than the practice by which one gets there. This is well illustrated, although it may not be immediately obvious to the reader, by the ceremonial opening of the Temple in the workings of a modern Rosicrucian Order. The Temple is symbolically separated from the outside world, and the participants identify themselves and their particular roles, and when this is done the sentence is proclaimed: 'Silence in the mouth of the Almighty One.' In the silence that follows, recollection is more important than practice.

This example also brings us to the question of ritual and its place in mystical experience. 'Respectable' ritual, as exemplified by public religious worship, has always been acceptable as a stimulus to religious and mystical experience; it does, after all, provide a near perfect setting for believers: the perfect proportion and symmetry of a Gothic cathedral which engages the aesthetic sense; the sensory stimulus provided by incense, plain chant, and ranks of lit candles, contrasted with the surrounding shadows and echoes of the chant; all of these stimulate the sense of awe that we call the *mysterium tremendum* and enable the worshippers to open themselves to the Divine Presence. Today, however, such a setting is all too rare – but if instead of an orthodox religious ritual one suggests that similar experiences can result from participation in an esoteric ceremony, there is no acceptance; the popular reaction is one of hostility: a compound of outrage at the flouting of orthodoxy, fear at the unknown, and envy of its potential for spiritual exaltation. Nor is this attitude likely to change until unorthodox forms of western spirituality are accepted for what they are rather than rejected for what they are not.

And yet for those drawn to it, esoteric ceremonial can be highly effective in exalting one to the mystical state. In the West the majority of Orders in which such ceremonies are worked are based on a symbolic ascent of the Tree of Life, which is itself a symbol of attainment to Divine Union. The ten stages on the Tree – the ten Sephiroth – are represented by ceremonies designed to raise the initiate to a state of consciousness appropriate to the spiritual state represented by each Sephirah. This is not the place to engage in a detailed examination of such work, but suffice it to say that in practice one *does* rise; not to the level of the Absolute, but perhaps to a vision of the Divine, even to a fleeting awareness of Divine Union, although only the vaguest of memories persist when the experience has passed.

This experiential limitation should be kept in mind from the outset by those who are called to follow this way, and more than others who follow different paths they should remember also that the practice is nothing; it is awareness of attainment that is all, for it is the awareness that is carried back into the outside world, and the awareness that leads us to the way of service that is the reward of attainment.

There are, of course, many non-ritual techniques for following the Mystic Way, and many of these have been correlated in *A Map of Mental States* (1983), a remarkable book by the psychologist John Clark. He converts Patanjali's Yoga meditation procedure into that most western of artefacts, the flow-chart; and he draws startling parallels between Richard of St Victor's 'Four Degrees of Passionate Love'; the four stages of prayer set out by St Teresa of Avila; and the ten 'Oxherding Pictures' (which set out in visual, symbolic form the path to enlightenment) of the Zen Master, Ka-kuan. Each of the ways to which he refers can also be related to his own structuring of the stages on the mystical path: Attachment, Disillusionment, Orientation, Concentration, Meditation with effort, Contemplation, Return to the Origin, Re-emergence, and Enlightenment. Whether these ten stages, and the ten Oxherding pictures, can be structurally related to the Sephiroth is an intriguing question. Perhaps a tenfold division of spiritual experience is an innate human activity, related to our physical structure and our natural tendency to count in tens; but there is, as we shall see, another, more significant aspect to Clark's analysis of the mystic way.

Whatever path is followed, the immediate end is the same – a direct, personal awareness, in vision or in union, of God, however we understand his nature and his essence. But there is a further goal to which the mystic eventually comes; the mystical path is not one of taking but of giving. At first one gives up attachment to the world, then one gives up the self, and at the last one gives up God – in order to give oneself, in whatever way one is guided, to mankind. It is easy to write this and easier still to read it, but it is hard indeed to follow the Mystic Way to this end.

Waite spoke of being in 'a law of service' when returning from the mystical state, and this finds echoes in all of the mystics. It is also the conclusion of John Clark in his psychological analysis. We begin, he says, in the average state, A, and progress by stages to enlightenment. But then: 'Perhaps there is a step beyond enlightenment, back to the Average State? . . . Indeed the whole point of the mystical path appears to be to help people back to A, back to being human again. It helps people to 'become what they are'. Enlightened people can tell where a person is on the mystical path because they have been along it themselves.'(p. 36.)

Just so, and it is then that their real work begins. This is true saintliness, the source of true inspiration and regeneration – not only of the individual but of all mankind. Certainly the purpose of mysticism has been seen in this light. Evelyn Underhill wrote (concerning the mystic life) that:

The power of living such a life depends upon organic adjustments, psychic changes, a heightening of our spiritual tension; not on the mere acceptance of specific beliefs. Hence the true object of Christianity – hidden though it be beneath a mass of credal and ritual decorations – is the effecting of the changes which lead to the production of such mystics, such 'free souls': those profound psychic and spiritual adjustments, which are called in their totality 'Regeneration'.

(*The Mystic Way*, 1913, p. 33)

The mystic, however, does not lose sight of the individual. He may take up the burden of what Montague Summers called 'Mystical Substitution', by which he meant the fervent and heartfelt prayer through which the mystic seeks to take on himself the sufferings of another – sufferings which are harder to bear and more damaging to the bearer when they are spiritual doubt and emptiness, than when they are purely physical. This is why, says Summers, 'It were ill for the neophyte to hazard presumptuously and ignorantly a harder task than he is able to accomplish.' (*Occult Review*, Vol. 28, No. 4, Oct. 1918, p. 218.)

And here a brief digression is in order. Just as the neophyte cannot bear the stress of substituting himself for another, so the novice was advised to avoid the *sama* of the Sufis, the musical concert which could throw the hearers into ecstasy and overwhelm the untrained. This advice applies equally to all techniques that have the mystical experience as their goal; apart from those who are teaching the technique, all the members of a group should be at roughly the same stage of progress: the effects may not be dramatic but it can be (indeed, it invariably *is*) disruptive and disharmonious to have an inexperienced person, however eager and committed, within a meditative or ceremonial group. 'Make haste slowly' is a good motto to adopt.

To return to the question of purpose. The lama who gains enlightenment and retains compassion will become not a Buddha, but a Bodhisattva – renouncing non-existence for himself in order to rescue others from the misery of circling on the wheel of rebirth. This, too, is mystical substitution. And it may be universally applied: 'The gospel of mercy', wrote A.E. Waite, 'is with us, in us, by us, and we can bring it into manifestation everywhere. This is the mystic's work in the world. It is in this sense that we are meant to be saviours of the whole society of Nature.' (*The Way of Divine Union*, 1915, p. 323.)

Nor has this sense of the mystic's mission been lost today. It is expressed clearly in Ursula King's *Towards a New Mysticism* (1980), in which she states:

> A Mysticism of action can inspire the spiritualisation of man in and through the unification of the world in all areas of becoming. The ascent of man is more than an ascent to knowledge. Humankind is called to the height of the spirit but no one can reach this summit on their own, in separation from others.
>
> (p. 232)

But although his path ends in union, and his return to the world is with the purpose of bringing that union – both in the world and out of it – to others, the mystic never truly finishes his quest. Arthur Machen 'once saw a little glint of the secret, merely a flash of the great radiance', and although he never forgot it, he knew that in truth, 'We shall go on seeking it to the end, so long as there are men on the earth. We shall seek it in all manner of strange ways; some of them wise, and some of them unutterably foolish. But the search will never end.'

Notes and References

Preface

1. Milton's *Paradise Lost*, Book 1, 300–302: 'Thick as autumnal leaves that strow the brooks/In Vallombrosa, where th'Etrurian shades/High over-arch'd imbower.'

2. The Kabbalah is the systematic presentation of post-exilic Jewish mysticism. Much of it is concerned with an inner spiritual interpretation of the Pentateuch, the first five books of the Old Testament, but for practical purposes its most important part is the image of the Tree of Life – a symbolic representation of the relationship between God, Man and the created universe. This is divided into ten stages (called in Hebrew the Sephiroth) that symbolize the various qualities – good and bad – inherent in both human nature and Creation as a whole. These ten stages are also seen in four aspects corresponding to different levels of human activity and awareness, so that a symbolic ascent of the Tree in the course of meditation can take place on four distinct planes of consciousness – the four 'Worlds' of Kabbalism.

   There is also an additional, or 'hidden' sephirah known as Daath (Knowledge), which can be seen as a meeting point of the masculine and feminine principles of God. In the third 'World', that of Briah or Creation, an experience of Daath is considered to be the highest point of awareness open to the human soul; for the Christian Kabbalist it can be described as an awareness of Paradise.

3. The Revd Alan Bain. See his *The Keys to Kabbalah*, 1989, p. 42.

Introduction

1. W.R. Inge (1860–1954) Dean of St Paul's and authority on Christian Mysticism in general, and on Plotinus in particular.

CHAPTER 1. MYSTICISM IN THE NON-CHRISTIAN WORLD

1. Louis-Claude de Saint-Martin (1743–1803), French mystic, known as 'Le Philosophe Inconnu' – the 'Unknown Philosopher'.

2. The term 'Mysteria' applied originally to specific religious festivals at Athens, but it gradually came to encompass the festivals of other cults associated with particular places, deities or heroes: thus the Eleusinian, Orphic, Dionysian and Bacchic Mysteries, and the non-Greek Mysteries of Mithras, Isis, Cybele and others. In general, the term 'Mystery Religions' encompasses all of these. Essentially the Mysteries involved secret and sacred rituals of a dramatic nature that represent a particular myth cycle, the experience of which induces religious awe in the initiate and brings enlightenment to him.

3. The philosophy of Plotinus (205–270 AD), which derives from Plato, is generally known as Neo-Platonism. His work survives as the *Enneads*: fifty-four essays that were brought together by his disciple Porphry, who arranged them according to their subject-matter in six groups of nine. (Hence their name from the Greek *ennea* – nine).

4. Gnosticism (from the Greek word 'gnosis' – knowledge) is the term applied to a religious movement within Christianity that developed in the second century. The various strands of Gnosticism are identified by the sources from which they drew their beliefs: Judaism, Platonism, the Mystery Religions and eastern dualist religions such as Mithraism. (Dualism is the belief in equal and opposite forces of Good and Evil; eternally co-existent and represented by matter (evil) and spirit (good).) For the believer, the world – and all human bodies – are the creation of an evil deity, and the essential characteristic of Gnosticism is the need to acquire a saving knowledge of the way in which the divine spark trapped within the body can return to the World of Spirit. The Saviour who brought this knowledge to mankind was Christ, but seen as a spiritual being quite distinct from the physical body of Jesus of Nazareth.

5. Sankara, or Sankaracharya, eighth-century AD Indian Vedanta philosopher and mystic. He was a monist, that is, one holding that there is no ultimate distinction between God and the universe.

6. After Rumi, the last great Persian mystical poet was Nur al-Din 'Abd al-Rahman Jami, 1414–92.

CHAPTER 2. MYSTICISM IN THE WEST

1. St Bernard of Clairvaux (1090–1153) was both a mystic and a driving force of the Cistercian monastic order.

2. The plural form of the Hebrew noun *sefirah* is derived from the word *sappir* – sapphire – and indicates that the Sephiroth are scintillating reflections of the Glory of God. Contrary to popular opinion, the word has no connection with the Greek *sphaira*, or sphere. (The Kabbalah and the Tree of Life – see Notes in the Preface.)

3. One of the foremost 'Doctors of the Church', Augustine (354–430) is known not only for his theological works, but also for his remarkable autobiography, the 'Confessions', in which he sets out his beliefs and tells the story of his conversion and his mystical experiences.

CHAPTER 4. NON-RELIGIOUS MYSTICISM

1. The Swiss psychiatrist Carl Gustav Jung (1875–1961) criticised the concepts of Freud and developed his own theories of psychological types and of the nature of the unconscious. His most original concept was that of the Collective Unconscious: the idea that there are shared features of the unconscious minds of all people, in all cultures throughout history. These features are typified by the archetypes: images, such as that of God, held in common by all mankind which result in remarkable parallels between different types of symbolism (for example those of dreams and of alchemy; and the religious imagery of east and west).

2. Henry Vaughan (1622–95), Welsh poet, known as 'the Silurist; his twin brother was Thomas Vaughan, the alchemist, who died in 1666.

3. Sir Francis Younghusband (1863–1942), explorer, political administrator and leader of the British Mission to Tibet in 1903.

CHAPTER 5. ESOTERIC MYSTICISM

1. A.E. Waite (1857–1942) is best known for his many sympathetic historical and critical studies of esoteric subjects, for his

translations in this field and for the Tarot pack he designed. He was also a mystic in his own right and deserves to better known for his important and highly original works on mysticism, written with a degree of objectivity rarely found among mystics themselves.

2. Mrs Atwood (1871–1910), as Mary Anne South, produced the classic, if impenetrable, Victorian study of spiritual alchemy: *A Suggestive Inquiry into the Hermetic Mystery* (1850).

3. Mme de Steiger (Isabelle de Steiger, 1836–1927) English artist and spiritual alchemist. She was the Elishah to Mrs Atwood's Elijah.

4. The Rosicrucians – if they had any historical reality, which is far from certain – were a quasi-religious order of esoteric philosophers, dedicated to spreading a true spiritual reformation and to healing the sick. They first came to public notice in the early seventeenth century with the appearance of three pamphlets (the so-called Rosicrucian Manifestos) that set out the story of their legendary founder, Christian Rosencreuz – from whom their name is derived – together with a summary of their history, aims and doctrines. In the ensuing controversy over the question of their reality, their cause was espoused by many of the 'Spiritual Alchemists' of the time – Thomas Vaughan among them.

CHAPTER 6. FALSE MYSTICISM

1. The Native American Church was legally incorporated in 1922 to preserve and promote the religious beliefs and practices of American Indian tribes in the South-Western United States. The sacramental eating of peyote in which its adherents – numbering some 250,000 – participate is built upon a foundation of both Christian and aboriginal myths.

2. Magic, that is, as it is popularly understood. I am well aware that there is another, more spiritually responsible approach in which the term 'magic' is applied to ritual activities of the highest spiritual quality, whose practitioners maintain – with justice – that a true knowledge of the self, which they gain from such practices, is important in order to be able more fully to serve mankind.

BIBLIOGRAPHY

This is not a comprehensive bibliography of either texts or studies, but an introductory guide for the reader who wishes to learn more of the literature of and on mysticism in all its forms.

REFERENCE WORKS AND ANTHOLOGIES OF TEXTS

Ferguson, John *An Illustrated Encyclopaedia of Mysticism and the Mystery Religions*, Thames & Hudson, 1976.

A good general guide but far from complete: among others the author omits both Coleridge and Evelyn Underhill.

Happold, F.C. *Mysticism, a Study and an Anthology*, Penguin, 1963.

A carefully chosen and sensitively annotated anthology that complements an excellent introduction to the subject.

Kingsland, William (ed.) *An Anthology of Mysticism and Mystical Philosophy*, Methuen, 1927.

Arranged under topical headings which are useful if a little idiosyncratic.

Nicholson, D.H.S. & Lee, A.H.E. (ed.) *The Oxford Book of English Mystical Verse*, OUP, 1916.

Heavily weighted in favour of the nineteenth century.

O'Brien, Elmer, S.J. *Varieties of Mystic Experience*, An Anthology and Interpretation, Mentor New York, 1965.

Concerned almost exclusively with mystics of the Roman Catholic Church down to the seventeenth century.

Wakefield, G.S. (Ed.) *A Dictionary of Christian Spirituality*, SCM Press, 1983.

In many ways a disappointing work, but it refers to many minor figures and is useful in explaining technical terms.

WRITINGS OF THE MYSTICS: TEXTS, TRANSLATIONS AND SPECIFIC STUDIES

A selection of the works of individual mystics, confined to the more accessible in the western tradition and to a representative few from eastern traditions.

Payne, R.J. (ed.) *The Classics of Western Spirituality*, A Library of the Great Spiritual Masters. SPCK, 1983.

An extensive and important series of translations into English of Christian, Jewish and Islamic texts.

Muller, F. Max (ed.) *The Sacred Books of the East*, OUP, 1879–1910.

An invaluable series first published in the late nineteenth century and since reprinted. Although not specifically devoted to mystical texts, it is an important source for eastern spirituality.

Boehme, Jacob *The Way to Christ*, trans. by J.J. Stoudt, Harper, 1947.

The seven 'tracts' in this work are representative of Boehme and are, perhaps, more readable than his other works, the more important of which were republished in English translation by C.J. Barker, between 1909 and 1924.

Stoudt, J.J. *Sunrise to Eternity*, A Study in Jacob Boehme's Life and Thought, University of Pensylvania Press, Philadelphia, 1957.

Buber, Martin *Tales of the Hasidim*, 3 vols, Schocken New York, 1947–1948.

The classic collection of Hasidic stories.

The Cloud of Unknowing, translated into modern English by Clifton Wolters, Penguin, 1961.

Eckhart, Meister *Sermons and Treatises*, 2 vols, translated and edited by M. O'C. Walshe, Element Books, 1979–1987.

Ancelet-Hustache, Jeanne *Master Eckhart and the Rhineland Mystics*, Longmans, 1958.

Guenther, Herbert V. *Treasures on the Tibetan Middle Way*, Shambhala, Berkeley, 1976.

There is a plethora of Tibetan texts available now in the West; this one has the merit of a masterly introduction and texts that are readily comprehensible.

Jefferies, Richard *The Story of My Heart*, ed. by S.J. Looker, 1947

St John of the Cross *Complete Works*, 3 vols, trans. by E. Allison Peers, Burns & Oates, 1953.

Peers, E. Allison *Studies of the Spanish Mystics*, 3 vols, 2nd ed, SPCK, 1951–1960.

Julian of Norwich *The Revelations of Divine Love*, trans. by James Walsh, Clarke, 1961.

Molinari, Paul, S.J. *Julian of Norwich*, Longmans, 1958.

Patanjali *The Yoga Sutras*, trans. by Charles Johnston, Watkins, 1901.

This is not the most scholarly translation but it is readily available.

Plotinus *The Enneads*, trans. by Stephen MacKenna, 3rd edn, revised by B.S. Page, Faber, 1962.

Inge, W.R. *The Philosophy of Plotinus*, 3rd edn, 2 vols, Longmans, 1929.

Rumi, Jalal ud-din *Mathnawi-i manawi*, ed. & trans. in 8 vols by R.A. Nicholson, Gibb Memorial Trust, 1925–40.

A complete text and translation of one of the greatest of Sufi works.

Ruysbroeck, Jan van *The Spiritual Espousals*, trans. by Eric Colledge, Faber, 1952.

Wautier-d'Aygalliers, A. *Ruysbroeck the Admirable*, Dent, 1925.

Sankaracharya *The Bhagavad Gita with the Commentary of Sri Sankaracarya*, trans. by A.M. Sastri, TPS, 1897.

Scheffler, Johannes Angelus Silesius, *Selections from The Cherubinic Wanderer*, trans. with intro. by J.E. Crawford Flitch, Allen & Unwin, 1932.

This extraordinary seventeenth century mystical poet converted to Catholicism and thus provides an illuminating counterpoint to Boehme.

St Teresa of Avila *The Complete Works*, ed. and trans. in 3 vols by E. Allison Peers, 1946.

Although entitled 'complete' it does not include the 'Letters' which had been published in 4 vols by the Benedictines of Stanbrook Abbey, 1919–24.

Zohar The Book of Enlightenment, trans. and intro. by D. Chanan Matt, SPCK, 1983.

This is the most accessible translation although it should be noted that it consists of selections only; the most comprehensive translation into English is *The Wisdom of the Zohar, an Anthology of Texts* by I. Tishby, 3 vols, OUP, 1989.

CRITICAL STUDIES AND HISTORIES OF MYSTICISM

Again, this is only a selection. The number of critical works is immense and there is no comprehensive bibliography, although one useful guide which lists some 1500 titles (including texts as well as studies) is *Mysticism – a Select Bibliography* by U. Sharma and J. Arndt, (Waterloo, Ont., 1973). Among earlier bibliographies, the most valuable is printed in Evelyn Underhill's *Mysticism*.

Bucke, R.M. *Cosmic Consciousness*, A Study in the Evolution of the Human Mind, New York, Innes, 1901 (frequently reprinted).

A classic study, with a substantial collection of 'Instances of Cosmic Consciousness' gathered by Bucke.

Butler, Dom Cuthbert *Western Mysticism*, Constable, 1922.

Cox, Michael *Mysticism, The Direct Experience of God*, Aquarian, 1983.

Concerned almost exclusively with Christian mysticism.

Clark, John H. *A Map of Mental States*, RKP, 1983.

A highly original approach to mapping the structure of the human mind; there is a lengthy and sensitive discussion of mystical experience.

Coleman, T.W. *English Mystics of the Fourteenth Century*, Epworth Press, 1938.

Coxhead, Nona *The Relevance of Bliss*, A Contemporary Exploration of Mystic Experience, Wildwood House, 1985.

The text incorporates contributions from many current students of mysticism.

Cohen, J.M. & Phipps, J-F. *The Common Experience*, Rider, 1979.

Although concerned specifically with identifying the common elements of all religious faith and experience, it is relevant to an analysis of the mystical experience.

Dean, Stanley R. (ed.) *Psychiatry and Mysticism*, Chicago, Nelson & Hall, 1975.

Of the 26 contributions, one third deal with mysticism as such; the remainder are concerned with psychical research.

Farges, Mgr Albert *Mystical Phenomena Compared with their Human and Diabolical Counterfeits*, A Treatise on Mystical Theology, Burns, Oates, 1926.

Very much a sectarian approach, but valuable for its detailed accounts of phenomena associated with many obscure Catholic mystics.

Govinda, Lama Anagarika *Foundations of Tibetan Mysticism*, According to the Esoteric Teachings of the Great Mantra, Rider, 1959.

Not a strictly accurate title as it is concerned with Tibetan Buddhism in general, but it is still useful.

Hardy, Sir Alister *The Spiritual Nature of Man*. A Study of contemporary religious experience, OUP, 1979.

This pioneering work is now continued at the Alister Hardy Research Centre in Oxford.

James, William *The Varieties of Religious Experience*, A Study in Human Nature, Longmans Green, 1902 (frequently reprinted).

One of the most important of earlier critical studies

Jones, Rufus M. *Studies in Mystical Religion*, Macmillan, 1909.

A classic work that contains a detailed analysis of early Protestant mysticism.

—*The Flowering of Mysticism*, The Friends of God in the Fourteenth Century, New York, Macmillan, 1939.

Katz, Steven T. (ed.) *Mysticism and Philosophical Analysis*, Sheldon Press, 1978.

Ten essays by theologians and philosophers.

King, Ursula *Towards a New Mysticism*, Teilhard de Chardin and Eastern Religions, Collins, 1980.

Laski, Marghanita *Ecstasy*. A Study of some Secular and Religious Experiences, Cresset Press, 1961.

—*Everyday Ecstasy*, Thames & Hudson, 1980.

A sequel to the previous work, considering also minor ecstatic experiences in the context of the secular world.

Lossky, Vladimir *Mystical Theology of the Eastern Church*, Clark, 1957.

Masters, R.E.L. & Houston, Jean *The Varieties of Psychedelic Experience*, Turnstone, 1966.

Inge, W.R. *Christian Mysticism*, Methuen, 1899.

A classic study incorporating careful historical and structural analyses.

Nicholson, Reynold A. *The Mystics of Islam*, RKP, 1914 (reprinted).

Otto, Rudolf *The Idea of the Holy*, An Inquiry into the Non-rational factor in the Idea of the Divine and its relation to the Rational, OUP, 1923.

—*Mysticism East and West*, A Comparative Analysis of the Nature of Mysticism, MacMillan, 1932.

In this work Otto concentrates largely on Eckhart & Sankara.

Ornstein, Robert E. (ed.) *The Nature of Human Consciousness*, A Book of Readings, Chicago, Freeman, 1973.

Parrinder, Geoffrey *Mysticism in the World's Religions*, Sheldon Press, 1976.

Scharfstein, Ben-Ami *Mystical Experience*, Oxford, Blackwell, 1973.

Somewhat flawed by an over-broad definition of mysticism and a readiness to accept unsoundly based theories.

Schimmel, Annemarie *Mystical Dimensions of Islam*, Chapel Hill, University of North Carolina Press, 1975.

Scholem, Gershom *Major Trends in Jewish Mysticism*, Schocken, New York, 1946.

The best-known of his studies, all of which are valuable although they assume a certain knowledge of Hebrew.

Stace, W.T. *Mysticism and Philosophy*, MacMillan, 1961.

An important critique of philosophical arguments about mysticism.

Suzuki, D.T. *Mysticism: Christian and Buddhist*, Allen & Unwin, 1957.

A comparative study that takes Eckhart as an archetypical Christian mystic – a somewhat unfortunate choice.

Tart, Charles T. (ed.) *Altered States of Consciousness*, Doubleday, Garden City, 1972.

Thirty-five papers under eight headings.

Thurston, Herbert, S.J. *The Physical Phenomena of Mysticism*, Burns Oates, 1952.

The standard study of this aspect of mysticism. It is much superior to a work with the same title by Montague Summers.

Underhill, Evelyn *Mysticism*, A Study in the Nature and Development of Man's Spiritual Consciousness, Methuen, 1911 12th edn revised, 1930).

The great classic study of mysticism; it is essential reading for any true understanding of the subject.

—*The Mystic Way*, A Psychological Study in Christian Origins, Dent 1913.

Von Hugel, Baron Friedrich *The Mystical Element of Religion* as studied in Saint Catherine of Genoa and her Friends, 2nd edition, Dent, 1923.

Of much wider application than is apparent from the title.

Waite, A.E. *The Way of Divine Union*, being a Doctrine of Experience in the Life of Sanctity, considered on the Faith of its Testimonies and Interpreted after a New Manner, Rider, 1915.

—*Lamps of Western Mysticism*, Essays on the Life of the Soul in God, Kegan Paul, 1923.

Despite their peculiarities of language and style, Waite's two studies of mysticism contain remarkable insights into the very essence and meaning of the mystic experience. He is the most lucid of what I term 'esoteric' Christian mystics.

Woods, Richard (ed.) *Understanding Mysticism*, Athlone, 1980.

A collection of thirty-six essays and extracts from other studies.

Zaehner, R.C. *Mysticism Sacred and Profane*, An Inquiry into some Varieties of Praeternatural Experience, OUP, 1961.

Incorporating a critical analysis of Huxley's experiments with mescalin.

—*Drugs, Mysticism and Make-believe*, Collins, 1972.

A number of books referred to, or quoted from in the text are not listed above; publication details for them will be found where reference to them is first made.

INDEX